The Whiskey Rebellion: Southwestern Pennsylvania's Frontier People Test the American Constitution

Jerry A. Clouse

MITCHELL COLLEGE LIBRARY
437 PEQUOT AVENUE
NEW LONDON, CT 06320

A publication of the
Commonwealth of Pennsylvania
Bureau for Historic Preservation
Pennsylvania Historical and Museum Commission
Harrisburg, 1994

**THE PENNSYLVANIA
HISTORICAL AND MUSEUM
COMMISSION**

Robert P. Casey
GOVERNOR

Kurt D. Zwikl
CHAIRMAN

COMMISSIONERS
Frank S. Beal
Michael E. Bortner, *Senator*
Bernard J. Dombrowski
Robert H. Fowler, Sr.
Constance Glott-Maine
Ann N. Greene
William F. Heefner
Edwin G. Holl, *Senator*
Stephen R. Maitland, *Representative*
LeRoy Patrick
James R. Roebuck, *Representative*
Anna Rotz
Donald M. Carroll, Jr., Ex Officio
Secretary of Education

Brent D. Glass
EXECUTIVE DIRECTOR

Brenda Barrett
DIRECTOR, BUREAU FOR
HISTORIC PRESERVATION

©1994
Commonwealth of Pennsylvania

ISBN 0-89271-057-8

Table of Contents

Introduction...1
    Memory of the Whiskey Rebellion
Significance..6
    National Significance
    Significance on the Frontiers of America
    Significance of Whiskey and Whiskey Distilling
Causes..12
    Underlying Factors
A Setting for Rebellion..19
    Synopsis of Events
Action!..25
    Open Rebellion Begins
    The Peace Process
    Epilogue
Footnotes to first section..44
Map of Seven-County Study Area...47
Guide to Associated Sites and Remaining Buildings....................................49
Footnotes to second section..75
Index..77

This publication has been financed entirely with Federal funds from the National Park Service, Department of the Interior. However, the contents and opinions do not necessarily reflect the views or policies of the Department of the Interior, nor does the mention of trade names or commercial products constitute endorsement or recommendation by the Department of the Interior. Under Title VI of the Civil Rights Act of 1964 and Sectuion 504 of the Rehabilitation Act of 1973, the U.S. Department of the Interior prohibits discrimination on the basis of race, color, national origin, or handicap in its federally assisted programs. If you believe you have been discriminated against, or if you desire further information, please wite to: Office for Equal Opportunity, U.S. Department of the Interior, Washington, DC 20240.

Acknowledgments

The author wishes to acknowledge the America's Industrial Heritage Project of the National Park Service for the grant awarded to the Pennsylvania Historical and Museum Commission which enabled this study of the Whiskey Rebellion. This examination of the Whiskey Rebellion is one segment of the Albert Gallatin Project, the goal of which is to research and interpret the life and times of Gallatin, as well as his role in and influence on southwestern Pennsylvania between 1780 and 1830. This fifty-year period coincides with his ownership of property in Fayette County, during which roads were developed, agriculture blossomed, and industry took hold in the region.

In addition, I would like to thank members of the Whiskey Rebellion Bicentennial Steering Committee for their enthusiasm in commemorating this vital link in America's political history and for providing me with contacts in each of the seven counties of this study. The interest of Roy Sarver of the Washington County Historical Society is much appreciated. Mark Ware of the Somerset Historical Center provided me with rich Somerset County sources. Historian Elizabeth Wall of Pittsburgh was notably helpful in locating Allegheny County records. PHMC librarian Carol Tallman was particularly efficient in locating hard-to-find sources. The comments and direction of Cornell University history professor Dorothy Fennell were especially helpful. I'm grateful to Kent Steinbrunner of Architectural Services for the creation of the map and value highly Kim Krammes's design and desktop publishing for this book. In addition, the editing by historians Louis Waddell and William Sisson, and Chief of the Division of Publications and Sales, Diane Reed, and by editor Harold Myers is much appreciated.

Introduction

Memory of the Whiskey Rebellion

Centered in southwestern Pennsylvania, the Whiskey Rebellion occurred in the summer and fall of 1794 when farmers, distillers, and artisans protested a federal excise tax on whiskey, through armed demonstrations. It had been three years since the hated excise law had been passed. Congress had been petitioned for repeal—excise collectors or their associates had been tarred and feathered, all to no apparent effect. When the U.S. Marshal appeared in the region with writs for noncomplying distillers to appear in U.S. Circuit Court in Philadelphia, it was too much to bear. A government which appeared insensitive to westerners' needs was now taking away their right to a trial in their vicinage. Violence broke out with the alleged killing of a protester by the Inspector of Revenue. The insurrection lasted only about eight weeks, but it was a tense period for the nation as it teetered on the brink of civil war.

I began research on the Whiskey Rebellion in April 1990. Since that time I've learned that the Whiskey Rebellion continues to be a controversial subject, especially in the seven-county region of my study: Bedford, Somerset, Fayette, Westmoreland, Allegheny, Washington, and Greene. I've also learned few sources agree as to whether the central government sparked the insurrection or whether the farmers/distillers of southwestern Pennsylvania were a mob gone berserk. In addition, there are still questions as to the role and significance of some of the major players in the Rebellion. As a member of the Whiskey Rebellion Task Force Steering Committee, I've witnessed heated discussions as to where the Rebellion actually took place. Some members from Washington and Allegheny counties didn't think Bedford County had any role in it.

Most scholars agree that the Whiskey Rebellion involved more than just southwestern Pennsylvania: it was a frontier-wide experience. For example, although no excise tax could be collected in Kentucky due to resistance, no governmental officials there dared to prosecute the violators of the law. In fact that is why the administration of President Washington took the rebellion so seriously and acted so swiftly in putting it down. Southwestern Pennsylvania happened to be closer to the capital than any of the other trouble spots.

In 1794 the young nation was still wrestling with its very identity—what the roles of a democratic government and its people should be. Among these were: (1) the role and responsibility of congressional representatives to their constituents and (2) the limits of Americans' rights as citizens. The Whiskey Rebellion served to draw public attention not only to the inequity of the whiskey excise but also to economic inequality generally as the frontier economy developed.

In doing research and survey work in each of the seven counties, I contacted as many local historians as time would allow. It was fascinating to observe the reactions of southwestern Pennsylvanians to the subject. Their perception and knowledge of the events were truly astonishing to me. Although areas of central Pennsylvania were also involved in the Rebellion, I'm sure few people of that region would be able to tell me where local events occurred that related to the Rebellion. On the other hand, in each of the seven southwestern counties local historians could relate where the federal army had marched or encamped, where a rebel had lived, or where a liberty pole had been erected.

Over time, myths and folklore have arisen concerning the people and places involved. Perceptions of the events have changed with the appearance of various writings on the subject. In fact, a possible reason that the people of southwestern Pennsylvania have remained so familiar with the Whiskey Rebellion story is that well-read histories and popular novels continued to be written about the subject in the region throughout the nineteenth and early twentieth century. Generally, it was the Federalist view which dominated historical writing on the subject from the time of the event until the early twentieth century. Immediately following the Rebellion, some of the leading participants wrote, to varying degrees, about their roles in this historic event. The writings of these politicians appear self-serving in their effort to clarify and substantiate their motives and actions. However, each had a different leadership role or participated in different events, and these are reflected in their various perspectives. Among these politicians were President George Washington, Treasury Secretary Alexander Hamilton, and Judge Alexander Addison, each representing the Federalist view, and State Representative Albert Gallatin, lawyer Hugh Brackenridge, and Congressman William Findley, each of whom generally promoted the Republican cause. Each was striving to make his recollection of Whiskey Rebellion events the defining memory of the nation.

View of Pittsburgh in 1790 showing Fort Pitt from across the Monongahela River and Grants Hill in the background.

By the 1790s, Brackenridge had become a bitter enemy of the Federalist Neville connection, a group of Pittsburgh's politically well-connected and prosperous men, and his writing about the insurrection quickly followed its termination. As an introduction to his book, Brackenridge wrote,

> *What I write is with a view to explain my own conduct which has not been understood. It is possible I may not be able to remove the misconception of every one. I am aware how difficult it is to change opinion, even with the best cause on my side: But I may support those who have undertaken my defence in conversation; and it may satisfy others, who are disposed to find men innocent rather than criminal.(1)*

The political rivalry continued into succeeding generations when Neville's grandson, Neville B. Craig, disparaged Brackenridge in his 1850s history of Pittsburgh. Consequently, Brackenridge's son Henry countered with another history which rectified his father's role in the Rebellion. This struggle over the interpretation and memory of the Whiskey Rebellion represents and typifies the deep internal political struggle of the region from its earliest colonial days through the post-

Revolutionary period.

In January 1795 John Scull, editor of *The Pittsburgh Gazette*, wrote in regard to the Whiskey Rebellion "that it may be handed down from one generation to another, to think and speak with horror of those who were the beginners of the late unfortunate calamity." As previously mentioned, it was the Federalist interpretation that dominated most histories of the Rebellion. This is one reason why it has largely been stowed away as a minor incident in early American history. The brief account the histories of western Maryland give of the event emphasize that the Maryland rebel faction was composed of the ignorant rabble of towns as well as the countryside who had been influenced by the "Whiskey Boys" of western Pennsylvania. The predominant view is that after the Revolution, Americans settled down to making a government in which all agreed to its form and function. The Whiskey Rebellion demonstrates how close the United States came to civil war because of the actual difference in philosophy.(2)

George Washington became the major symbol of the Revolutionary era. In most of Pennsylvania what is known about the Whiskey Rebellion revolves around where George Washington stopped, where he ate, where he worshipped, where he stood. On the southwest side of the Harris Mansion on Front Street in Harrisburg is a large, flat brownstone. On its surface are inscribed the words, "Washington October 3, 1794." It was on this stone that Washington stood to accept the praises of Harrisburg Burgesses Bombach and Berryhill as he stopped on his way west to review the troops. In Carlisle, five Pennsylvania Historical and Museum Commission markers note where Washington reviewed the troops, where he lodged, where his staff stayed, and where he worshipped. In addition, historical markers commemorate his stops in Reading and Chambersburg.(3)

Southwestern Pennsylvania has a more complex memory of the Rebellion. In the heart of the political turmoil of the 1790s, it felt the sting of Washington's march. It not only remembers where George Washington slept, but also where men or whiskey were hidden at the approach of the army. Historian David Thelan asserts, "People develop a shared identity by identifying, exploring, and agreeing on memories." He also finds that "the struggle for possession and interpretation of memory is rooted in the conflict and interplay among social, political, and cultural interests and values in the present." After two hundred years, the majority of residents no longer feel guilt or remorse for the event, but instead believe that the rebels were justified in their actions. Although based on the original memory of the Rebellion, the current memory of the Rebellion has changed to reflect the proud and independent heritage of the region.(4)

When asked about Bedford's role in the Rebellion, local historian Vaughn Whisker replied that the most important event was the encampment of seven thousand troops at the Irondale Hotel, on the southeastern edge of Bedford Borough, now the Elks Club Golf Course.(5) Bill Defibaugh, an architect living in Bedford, remembered fragments of stories of his family's involvement in the event. He had been told that both the Brumbaugh distillery near Morrison's

Cove in St. Clair Township and the Defibaugh distillery were burned by the federal troops. Both were re-established after the Rebellion. He said both the Defibaugh brothers served jail terms—albeit short ones. (Jacob and Adam Defibaugh were charged with treasonous activities in 1794.)(6)

Canon Richard Davies, Episcopalian clergyman and member of the Whiskey Rebellion Bicentennial Committee, said that during the 1790s the area of Chartiers Creek was the most sophisticated in the region due to men like the Federalists John Neville and Isaac Craig, who lived there. They were founding members of St. Luke's Episcopal Church. After the Rebellion, this church declined in membership and the building fell into disrepair because the farmers of the area wanted to have nothing to do with anything associated with Neville. The present stone church was erected in 1852, and a plaque placed there by the Pennsylvania Society of the Colonial Dames in 1928, reads:

> *In honor of George Washington and John Neville, united in their ideals of an orderly government, co-workers in suppressing the Whiskey Insurrection, the only armed conflict of which occurred on a hill adjacent to this church.(7)*

I asked local historian Gilbert Balliard of Gastonville, Washington County, how the local area feels about the Whiskey Rebellion. He replied that the Monongahela Chapter of the Daughters of the American Revolution and the Washington County Historical Society are all "hepped up" about it. He added, "For a long time it was a hushed-up affair around here." When he first joined Mingo Creek Presbyterian Church in 1924, you didn't mention it. These were tight-mouthed Presbyterians, and the old folks didn't like to hear about makin' whiskey. He remembers eighty-year-old B. F. McVay, a Sunday School teacher at Mingo, talking about Tom the Tinker, reputed leader of whiskey rebels who attacked the stills of those who complied with the excise law. Balliard has no doubt John Holcroft was Tom the Tinker. "Holcroft was easily led by the crowd, but John Hamilton had a cool head."(8)

When Henry McCook wrote his historical novel, *The Latimers: A Tale of the Western Insurrection of 1794*, in 1897, he noted that the reputation of the Scotch-Irish had suffered for their association with it. In the foreword, he stated that he did

> *not seek to exempt the Scotch-Irishmen and others, associated directly or indirectly with the western riots, from deserved censure; but he believes that the character of the men censured, as well as their motives and the actual degree of criminality in the various risings, have been exaggerated and misrepresented in history, and are not understood by the people at large.(9)*

Irk McConnell, a descendant of Alexander McConnell, recalled that his ancestor "chased [the rebel leader] Bradford down the river." McConnell was a militiaman, and according to family tradition, he "rode Lyle to Philadelphia with a rope around his neck." Irk said that the Lyles were from Hickory, about six miles from the McConnell homestead. When questioned how McConnell's Federalist actions were viewed by his neighbors, Irk replied that the McConnells were quite influential in the area, owning a large tract of land and a grist and saw mill. Irk lives in the Alexander McConnell House, a two-and-one-half story, three-bay, stone house built in 1805. According to other records, Peter Lyle, an Allegheny County distiller, was one of the leaders of the attack on Bower Hill. He was later arrested and taken to Fort Fayette, from which he escaped. One of those who fled western Pennsylvania, Lyle was tried in absentia and was found guilty of treason. He was later pardoned.(10)

Miller Barb is a resident of Mapletown, Greene County. A descendant of John Minor, who was one of Greene Township's representatives at the Parkinson's Ferry meeting, Barb recalled that Minor was a friend of Rev. John Corbley. He said that Minor went along with Corbley back to Philadelphia. He also noted that the Minor brick house, east of town on the Whiteley Creek, was torn down and is now the site of a "state" dump.(11)

The memories of incidents and people may not always agree with written histories, but they show how personal the memories of the Rebellion continue to be for the families who lived there, and continue to live there. For example, descendants of Colonel Edward Cook, a leader of the moderate faction of rebels, have appeared on special occasions commemorating the Whiskey Rebellion, not only to honor their ancestor and the ancestral home but to express their enduring interest in the subject as well.

Beginning with Leland Baldwin's 1939 history of the Whiskey Rebellion, the whiskey rebel has been seen as something other than a rabble-rouser. Leading the research by social historians on the subject was R. Eugene Harper with his 1969 dissertation on the class structure of western Pennsylvania. Dorothy Fennell followed with her social history of the Rebellion in 1981. Thomas Slaughter built on these works and essentially wrote the intellectual history of the Rebellion in 1986.

I see my work as a continuation of trying to bring a balanced view of the Rebellion's history to the public. I've utilized the most recent interpretations of the Rebellion, included a few of my own insights, and have gone back to the contemporary writings to hear what the participants and observers had to say. However, there are still things unknown about how the various political, economic, and cultural forces affected the people and their leaders of late eighteenth-century America. In addition, this book provides the only known guide to Whiskey Rebellion associated sites in the seven-county region.

Silhouette of John Neville.

Significance

National Significance of the Whiskey Rebellion

The Whiskey Rebellion is significant in American history as the first test of the American Constitution and the laws established by it. Armed opposition to the due process of law became equivalent to treason. Federal judiciary power was strengthened and state regulations weakened proportionately. The Rebellion set a precedent for the power of the chief executive to nationalize militia forces. Through its actions the national government emphasized the frontier, the interior regions of the nation, as a priority for settlement and containment within the union of states.

Some historians argue that the Rebellion was the last violent battle over the meaning of the American Revolution. Even two decades after 1776, Americans were still fighting about taxes, circulating petitions of protest, and forming political action societies to defend the liberties they believed they had won earlier. The 1790s were a time of upheaval and transformation in the long process of changing American politics from a system based upon British colonialism to a republican system. The coalitions of the 1770s gave way to partisanship in legislative and electoral politics. The government's response in the form of troops and court proceedings spurred the birth of the Republican and Federalist parties. Although the rebels lost this fight, they soon learned that the best avenue for political change is through the ballot box.(12)

This young nation, made up of different peoples with diverse backgrounds, only appeared to have a shared political ideology to unite it. Actually, there were two predominant conceptions of democracy: the Federalists favored a hierarchical society with limited access to government by the common man, while the Republicans preferred open and equal access to government by all. The Whiskey Rebellion illustrated that American nationalism based on either ideology was both powerful and exceedingly fragile. Both the short- and long-term results of the Whiskey Rebellion illuminated two key elements in the democratic process: one, the balancing of power and philosophies through elections, and two, compromising for the good of the majority. Many Americans realized that patriotism had to be transformed into inspirational symbols and images. American nationality came to be personified in George Washington, who not only reviewed and led the federal troops west to quell the Rebellion but also drew homage from the people along the way. The Rebellion also drew American attention to the West with its seemingly boundless prospects. The Whiskey Rebellion fertilized the seeds of republican ideals, while their great proponent, Thomas Jefferson, would soon focus the nation's attention on its interior regions.(13)

Significance of Insurrection or Rebellion on the Frontiers of America

Insurrections and protests occurred on the American frontier, previous to the Whiskey Rebellion. What became known as the War of the Regulation occurred in North Carolina in the early 1770s. Farmers and artisans of the backcountry of this state became greatly dissatisfied with a corrupt government whose leaders were concerned only with the welfare of the merchant-lawyer-office-holding elite. These sycophants largely lived in the eastern coastal area of the state and perpetuated their office through high taxes and restrictive laws on the largely agrarian residents of the backcountry. Although the government was petitioned, it was heedless to the calls of reform. Finally, armed regulators attacked courts of session, often holding them hostage or disbanding them. This prompted the governor to raise troops. The conflict ended in armed confrontation between the state's troops and the shoddily armed insurrectionists. Of course the government troops were equal to the challenge, and the regulators were dispersed. Some of the leaders were hanged, but one of them, Herman Husband, fled to Pennsylvania, where this training and his Revolutionary experience would be used twenty years later in the Whiskey Rebellion.(14)

Another frontier insurrection has been termed Shays' Rebellion of 1786-87. This occurred on the frontier of Massachusetts where disgruntled farmers struggled for economic relief. As in the North Carolina case, the farmers and artisans in western Massachusetts were facing economic conditions different from their eastern brethren. The farmers began their protest with petitions and conventions to make their governmental representatives aware of their distress. Instead of making changes favorable to the farmer, however, laws were made to increase the power and holdings of the commercial/political elite. When the farmers' reform efforts failed, they took up guns and formed groups and called themselves regulators after their North Carolina predecessors. They took courts hostage, in particular debtor courts, as had their counterparts in the Carolinas.(15)

Cartoon of an excise officer being pursued by two farmers, who intend to tar and feather him.

Instead of government officials getting the point that the farmers were in economic distress, they saw the farmers as plotting their own rise to power. Those who had been Revolutionary leaders feared extralegal/popular protests and met the Shaysites with military force. They raised an army, which served to radicalize the farmers, who continued to maraud political, military, and commercial leaders after they had officially been defeated by the Governor's armed forces. Many of the insurgents fled to the Ohio Valley, which served as a haven for the rebels and provided a means to end the rebellion without a final confrontation. The bulk of Shaysites, however, remained in Massachusetts, where they continued the fight by opposing the federal Constitution.(16)

Many similarities can be seen between Shays' Rebellion and the

Whiskey Rebellion. Most of the Shaysites were of English or Scotch-Irish ancestry and members of the Congregational Church. Many of the whiskey rebels were Scotch-Irish and members of the Presbyterian Church. The social uniformity of these groups enhanced unity and facilitated communication between individuals and communities. This is why it was possible for whiskey rebels to be meeting August 14, 1794 at Parkinson's Ferry in Washington County and on the same date in Cumberland County. There was a high literacy rate in Pennsylvania during the 1790s, and letters, broadsides, and newspapers were passed from neighbor to neighbor or read in the local tavern. Historian Joseph Ellis notes that the backcountry counties of Pennsylvania had a literacy rate of sixty-five percent which compared with a sixty percent literacy rate in England and fifty percent in France. Similarly, Baptist groups in southwestern Pennsylvania were served by itinerant preachers who spread protest information from congregation to congregation. And the German Brethren groups of Somerset County were composed of tight-knit families, which facilitated communication there as well.(17)

Other similarities include the fact that these rebellions were regional clashes of eastern mercantile interests against western agrarian interests. Both can be seen as clashes between traditional societies and developing commercial cultures. Disgruntled Revolutionary War soldiers were major players in both conflicts. Although many Shaysites and whiskey rebels fled into the Ohio Valley, many also stayed as the economic prospects in their regions brightened after the conflict eased. The release of these people onto the frontier relieved economic pressure and prevented a prolonged guerilla war.

The history of the excise protest has its antecedents in the Stamp Act crisis of 1765 and earlier excise protests in Great Britain in the seventeenth and eighteenth centuries. The earliest protest incident in southwestern Pennsylvania occurred in 1786 when excise officer William Graham appeared in Washington County only to be attacked and humiliated. This last episode marked the end of the state excise in the western counties of Pennsylvania until the federal government passed a new excise bill in March 1791. Frontier farmers hated the tax on whiskey because it struck at their most valuable market commodity in what was essentially a local barter economy. Used as a measure of value, a gallon of whiskey in western Pennsylvania stores was equivalent to a shilling. In 1798 tax assessor James Irwine of Westmoreland County disparaged John Young's log cabins by declaring, "I believe them not worth one gill of whiskey." Simply put, there wasn't cash for the necessities of life, let alone any for an obnoxious tax. The tax had completely disrupted the frontier farmers' economy just as it was emerging commercially. The excise tax spelled disaster for domestic manufacture by the small producer.(18)

The enactment of this tax stirred the ire of frontiersmen and brought to light a multitude of problems facing them: the decreasing opportunity to own land, the lack of access to markets, the lack of military protection, and eastern elitism. It also brought attention to the American frontier as a separate place where hardship was an everyday experience. Washington considered the frontier the most crucial element in the survival of the United States. This frontier was not only important in national politics but in international politics as well. An independent frontier nation that could fall into the hands of Great Britain or Spain was an odious thought. This was one reason President Washington raised more troops to put down the Whiskey Rebellion than were ever raised to fight the Indians on the frontier and more than any force he had commanded during the American Revolution.(19)

The Whiskey Rebellion appears to have been inevitable, in that by this time two fundamentally different views of the American Revolution and the American Constitution had developed. Whereas many Revolutionary leaders, such as George Washington, Alexander Hamilton, and Samuel Adams, saw the first conflict as necessary for them to gain greater control over American affairs, other leaders, such as Thomas Jefferson, saw the Revolution as a democratizing force by which all elements of American society would have an equal opportunity for material wealth, political office, and social privileges.(20)

Significance of Whiskey and Whiskey Distilling in Southwestern Pennsylvania

As previously mentioned, whiskey was the region's most valuable market commodity. During the 1780s, subsistence farming was predominant throughout this frontier region. However, by the 1790s farmers of the Monongahela Valley were able to farm commercially. According to local histories, the Monongahela Valley was particularly suited to the growing of rye grain. Although other grains or fruits could be used in the manufacture of whiskey, rye was predominantly used in western Pennsylvania. Agricultural historian Stevenson Fletcher notes that rye yields were somewhat higher than those of wheat, especially in poorer soils or land under indifferent management. Fletcher also reports that more rye was grown from the colonial period up to 1840 than barley or oats. This was particularly true during the period when the Hessian fly was scourging wheat fields. (The Hessian fly first appeared in Pennsylvania in 1786 and by 1797 had spread west of the Alleghenies.) English traveler Henry Wansey stated in 1794 that if more barley were cultivated and breweries established in America, the general use of whiskey would be lessened. He further reported that whiskey was the beverage of the frontier settlers because every man with a small still and a little rye could produce it in his own house. Fletcher attributed to William Strickland the 1801 statement that all the backcountry of America is very favorable to the growth of rye, and it is entirely consumed in the distillation of whiskey. During the late eighteenth and early nineteenth centuries, the distilling industry was inseparable from the farming industry and was universal throughout the rural districts of Pennsylvania.(21)

Whiskey in the late eighteenth century was not a luxury—it was a necessity. It was consumed on all occasions whether they were social, religious, or political. It was a particular requisite on the frontier because of the poor living conditions and the hard everyday physical labor. Whiskey was used for medicinal purposes just as aspirin is today. It was reportedly good for fevers, ague, and snakebite. According to one account, it was sometimes drunk with tansy, mint, or maple sugar, but it was primarily taken straight. Historical geographer James Lemon noted that the most demanding periods for the typical late eighteenth-century farmer were June and July, when hay was cut and small grains harvested. Associated with the harvest and hard work was the whiskey distributed to the field hands to ease their pain and fatigue. One of the most important duties of the military quartermaster was to requisition sufficient amounts of whiskey for the army's daily ration. During the march of the federal troops, drunkenness was widespread among the officers and enlisted men. The government spent huge sums in western Pennsylvania to supply the soldiers with food and whiskey.(22)

Political economist Tench Coxe wrote in 1810 that the American manufacture of spirits was principally from rye, apples, and peaches. Very little whiskey or liquor was imported at that time, most being produced in American distilleries. The large amount of rye produced for these distilleries helped keep the price of wheat high because it employed a disproportionate part of the cleared land and labor of the country, keeping wheat production low. Earlier figures cannot be found, but Pennsylvania in 1840 ranked number one in the United States in the production of rye.(23)

Although historian Leland Baldwin stated that about twenty-five percent of United States stills in 1794 were located in the Monongahela country, it may be more accurate to say twenty-five percent of the stills were in Pennsylvania. The earliest-known complete record is from Tench Coxe's 1810 list of manufactures. Coxe records thirty-six Pennsylvania counties with 3,594 distilleries. Of this number 799 or twenty-two percent were in southwestern Pennsylvania. (For unknown reasons Greene County was not listed as having distilleries.) Adam Seybert's 1818 *Statistical Annals* notes 14,191 stills in the United States in 1810. Accordingly, twenty-five percent of all United States stills were located in Pennsylvania. (Please note that these early records are often unreliable, but they are used here to give an idea of what may have existed at that time.)(24)

Although some southwestern Pennsylvania histories have stated that at the time of the Rebellion every fifth or sixth farm had a still, a look at the tax records indicates that this number is high. For example, using the tax records for Strabane Township, Washington County, 1791-93, there was a yearly average of 234 taxables in that township with a yearly average of fifteen stills. This would mean that approximately one in fifteen, or about seven percent of the taxable population, had stills. (R. Eugene Harper's study of Fayette County tax records shows a similar statistic of one in each fifteen to sixteen taxables having a still.) Dorothy Fennell in her studies determined that about eleven per cent of the western taxable population had stills. She also made a study of the role of the distiller in the Whiskey Rebellion. She found that only one in four rebels was a distiller. However, thirty percent of Washington County rebels owned stills.(25) The study of Strabane Township provides some documentation of the mobility or fluctuations in whiskey distilling in that county. Less than half of the distillers operated year after year. Comparison of these records with Neville's 1796-97 excise records revealed that less than a

third had been previously recorded with stills. The results of these comparisons show that late eighteenth-century stilling tended not to be a permanent occupation.(26)

The earliest stills in the region were rather simple "teakettle" affairs, constructed in all probability by local coppersmiths. Their nickname was taken from their shape. The size or capacity of the still was determined by the distiller, but generally ranged from 50 to 150 gallons. George Divers of Albemarle County, Virginia, advised Thomas Jefferson in 1793 "to purchase One Still that will work 85, one of 45, and a Copper Kettle of Sixty Gallons—with these Stills and Boiler you may make from 70 to 80 Gallons of whiskey p Week." Since cold water was essential in the distilling process, the still house was always located below a never-failing spring. Most were set up in temporary roof shelters erected mainly to protect the equipment and attendants from inclement weather, or in small log cabins. The simplicity in design of the still and its shelter was conducive to the mobility of this industry. Two distilleries which became among the largest and best known in the region were started in this fashion. They were the Overholt Distillery in South Huntingdon Township, Westmoreland County, and the Large Distillery in Mifflin Township, Allegheny County. Both began as small family operations in log buildings, but as the quality of their liquor became renowned, their buildings were expanded and production increased during the nineteenth and early twentieth centuries.(27)

A copper still from the Bedell Distillery, near Large Creek, Jefferson Borough, Allegheny County.

Neville's 1796-97 list of stills and stillers for Washington County shows 413 distillers with 602 stills. (This list comprised Greene County townships as well.) Somerset Township had the largest number of distillers at thirty-four, but Cumberland Township had the largest number of stills at fifty-five. The percentage of distillers with only one still within a township ranged from fifty to eighty per cent. Most of the still houses in Cumberland Township were of little monetary value. Only thirteen were substantial enough to be evaluated in the 1798 Direct Tax. Nevertheless, a few of these were larger than the owners' cabins.

Historians have reiterated that one of the burdens of the whiskey excise was the fact that whiskey had to be hauled over the Alleghenies at an added expense. William Hanna in his 1882 *History of Greene County* states that whiskey was put in kegs holding from six to twenty gallons. These kegs were then put in a wallet across the back of a packhorse. After twenty to thirty horses were thus fitted out, the company would head east. There is no doubt that hauling would have been an added expense, but there is little documentation as to how much of the whiskey manufactured in the Monongahela Valley was hauled over the mountains. On the other hand, documents found at the Westmoreland County Historical Society indicate that whiskey, maple sugar, and ginseng were being shipped down the Ohio River by 1793. Likewise, social historian R. Eugene Harper has found that by the 1790s the yeoman class, or about one-third of the western population, had developed commercial agriculture based on a growing downriver trade.(28)

A stronger assertion for the Ohio River trade is made by Pennsylvania historian S. K. Stevens, who states that by 1794, one hundred thousand gallons of whiskey were being exported down the Ohio. Additional testimony of how and where the whiskey of western Pennsylvania traveled is found in the newspapers of the era. A 1794 advertisement found in the *Carlisle Gazette* beckoned "for boatmen to go to New Orleans, clever fellows who may wish to engage, will apply to James Blaine in Carlisle." Although there were advertisements in the Philadelphia papers noting shipments of "Spanish Madeira, Jamaica rum, porte, etc.," there was none advertising the arrival of Pennsylvania or Monongahela whiskey. In July 1793 John and Charles Wilkins advertised in *The Pittsburgh Gazette* to pay cash for whiskey if the excise duties had been paid on it.(29)

British traveler Henry Toulmin wrote of Kentucky in 1793 that "till very lately a considerable portion of the spirits which are consumed in the state have been brought down the river from the settlements on the Monongahela." He also noted that "whiskey sells tolerable well among the American settlers at Natchez and other parts of West Florida and Louisiana, contiguous to the Mississippi." During the 1790s typical cargoes arriving on flatboats at Natchez included both whiskey and liquor stills. All this evidence indicates that not only did the western Pennsylvania whiskey travel by a western route but its market was principally in the rapidly expanding western frontier as well.(30)

Causes

Underlying Factors for Rebellion in Southwestern Pennsylvania

The Whiskey Rebellion occurred in the summer of 1794 when farmers of western Pennsylvania decided the laws of the nation had become too repressive for them to submit to. It had been three years since the hated excise law had been passed. The federal government, sitting east of the Alleghenies, appeared indifferent to the requirements of western farmer/distillers. When the U.S. Marshal appeared on the scene with writs for noncomplying distillers to appear in U.S. Court in Philadelphia, it was too much to bear. Armed protest was precipitated by the alleged killing of a protester by the Inspector of Revenue. Despite the fact that the insurrection was shortlived, it was the Washington administration's greatest crisis in setting and directing government policy.

Although it was more than a decade since the American Revolution had ended, the young nation was still attempting to resolve what the roles of the government and the people should be. Among these issues were the role and responsibility of congressional representatives to their constituents and the limits of Americans' rights as citizens. Indeed, the meaning of citizenship and the role of law and order in a democratic society were still being discussed at the national as well as local level. In a republican government, does good citizenship mean not only respecting its laws but also assembling and demonstrating alternative viewpoints on an unpopular law?(31)

Many of the leaders of the Revolution had come to realize that a centralized government was needed to effectively raise taxes and armies in order to protect the liberties thus gained. They believed that the loose confederation of states would soon fall prey to enemies within and without. Their efforts to correct this resulted in the Constitution of 1787. However, other men feared the power given to a centralized national government would prove to be oppressive and destructive of the people's liberties. These men formed the antifederalist party and worked to amend the Constitution. Although these men were effective in producing the Bill of Rights, added to the Constitution in 1791, they still had legitimate concerns about the direction of national government.

A combination of circumstances and issues made western Pennsylvania ripe for insurrection. The region west of the Alleghenies already had a long history of defying governmental authority. In the 1760s Governor John Penn had described the frontier people of western Pennsylvania as a "lawless ungovernable crew." Contentious would best describe the beginnings of local civil government in the region in the 1770s. Like the Pennsylvania-Virginia trade rivalry that had dominated the politics of the previous two decades, the question of whether Pennsylvania or Virginia should have governmental authority and control of the region commanded local political energies for the next two decades. This political factiousness carried over into the 1790s.(32) Not only did excise tax opponents dislike the financial burden of the tax, but they also feared the power it gave the national government. At the same time, the Rebellion was as much an internal crisis within the region as it was a confrontation between the United States government and the farmer/distillers.

Pennsylvania had been politically divided by region since the French and Indian War. It was during that conflict that the repeated calls for the defense of the frontier and the lack of action by the Assembly, sitting in Philadelphia, produced a lasting resentment. Indeed, it was only during the brief span of the Revolutionary War that a history of common resistance to the British Crown created a tenuous bond between the residents of eastern and western Pennsylvania. Distrust of an unresponsive government pervaded the frontier political identity into the 1790s. The Susquehanna River roughly divided the state into two regions. Southeastern Pennsylvania was dominated by mercantile, manufacturing, and landholding interests of old established families while western Pennsylvania was largely controlled by farmer/artisan immigrants and newcomers.(33)

Albert Gallatin wrote to his wife Hannah in 1795: "In Pennsylvania we have neither Livingstones nor Rensselaers, but from the suburbs of Philadelphia to the banks of Ohio I do not know a single family that has any extensive influence. An equal distribution of property has rendered every individual independent, and there is amongst us true and real equality." Author/lawyer Henry M. Brackenridge wrote of a trip across Pennsylvania in the early nineteenth century: "There is, perhaps no part of the world where there is so much wealth distributed among so many hands, and in equal proportions, as in Middle and Western Pennsylvania!" Only Pittsburgh shared in the commercial interests of the east. Whereas independence was enthusiastically supported by most western Pennsylvanians, southeastern Pennsylvania's involvement was hampered by segments of its population who were loyalists, reluctant rebels, or pacifists. Throughout the national and state political controversies of the 1780s, southeastern Pennsylvania and western Pennsylvania remained consistently opposed.(34)

Another force on the political scene was the French Revolution, which had begun in 1789. The events in France brought to the forefront the democratic ideal that it is the duty of the citizen to take an unceasing share in his government. Sympathy for the French swelled in America from the start. American friends of liberty not only drank toasts to their comrades at political and military gatherings, but also raised money and goods for the relief of Frenchmen. Dutch traveler Theophile Cazenove, on his journey in 1794 through New Jersey and Pennsylvania, saw high poles topped with a liberty bonnet and little boys with tricolored French ribbons in their hats. French Ambassador Edmund Charles Genet arrived in 1793 to recruit volunteers to aid his nation's cause. This was viewed by Washington as part of an international scheme against order, and he feared the contagion would spread to the west where the situation was already volatile.(35)

A prominent issue of these politically turbulent times was the defense of the frontiers. Western Pennsylvania continued to be a violent region with sporadic Indian attacks occurring into the 1790s. General Josiah Harmar's expedition against the Ohio Indians in 1790 met with defeat, and General Arthur St. Clair's ill-clad and ill-prepared force met an even worse defeat in 1791. These defeats not only left frontier settlers uneasy but peaked British and Spanish interest in inciting unrest on the American frontiers. The Indian threat to western Pennsylvania was finally broken on August 20, 1794, when General Anthony Wayne's forces defeated the Indians at the Battle of Fallen Timbers near present-day Toledo, Ohio. In each of these instances the army was composed of no more than fifteen hundred men whom it had taken months to assemble.(36)

Economics was another sore point for westerners. The promises of equality and freedom for which these people had fought during the Revolution seemed elusive. Eastern speculators appeared to have better opportunity to own the best land in the region. Increasingly in the 1790s it was harder for the average settler to own land—one of the reasons settlers were willing to face the hardships of frontier life in the first place. The government also appeared passive in opening the Mississippi for commerce, the only logical avenue of trade for people west of the Alleghenies. Despite having representatives in Congress, western interests did not appear to be taken into account. This was especially manifested in the passage of the excise tax, which seemed to be directed at those who depended on the manufacture of whiskey for a livelihood and those who could least afford to pay it. Westerners perceived injustice not only in the excise law itself, but also in the government's ignoring of their petitions against it.(37)

In the early 1790s, the communities along the Youghiogheny and

Monongahela rivers were in the initial stages of commercialization and industrialization. Iron-making, boat building, and whiskey distilling were changing the economy. More men were becoming laborers and artisans in these trades and occupations associated with them. In addition, many of the farmers had developed their farms to the point where commercial farming was possible. As towns and communities began to grow, the land along the rivers became more valuable. With increased prices and the specialization of jobs it was increasingly more difficult to be a subsistence farmer. During economic upturns, many marginal farmers and laborers moved further on into the frontier. As mentioned previously, those dissatisfied with their economic status often became participants in political upheavals.(38)

Another simmering issue was the fact that this was a separate region from the East. Even into the early nineteenth century, the trans-Appalachian counties of Pennsylvania were termed the "western country." The people west of the Alleghenies were not drawn naturally to Philadelphia for trade but instead looked to the Ohio and the Mississippi rivers for commerce. A letter from the *Kentucky Gazette* called for the "right to free navigation of the western waters" and an end to the "injustice done to the inhabitants of the West by the insidious policy of East America." In 1776 this region claimed by both Pennsylvania and Virginia petitioned for independence of both. The state of "Westsylvania" would not be created, but the issue would come alive again in 1794.(39)

In the 1790s the Mississippi River was transformed into a vital transportation link largely by three factors: the Spanish royal order of 1788 which encouraged American trade and immigration; the War of the First Coalition, pitting Spain against France 1793 to 1795, curtailing trade between Louisiana and Spain and promoting Louisiana's trade with the United States; and the large influx of population upriver, which brought statehood to Kentucky in 1792 and to Tennessee in 1796.(40)

The mixture of people themselves, with their religious and cultural ties and political ideals, was a contributing factor in the Rebellion. The greater part of the population, including English, Welsh, Irish, and Scotch-Irish, could trace its ancestry to the British Isles. However, there were other groups, the most numerous of which were the Germans and Swiss. Whatever their ethnic background, opportunities for cheap land and the freedom to live as they saw fit were the driving forces compelling the people to risk the arduous journey over the mountains.

Nearly one quarter of the inhabitants were of Scotch-Irish ancestry. Many were part of the great wave of immigration from Ulster in the 1770s just prior to the Revolution. They, along with earlier Scotch-Irish immigrants of the Cumberland Valley, contributed greatly to the rapid settlement of southwestern Pennsylvania after the Land Purchase of 1768. After the Revolution, they became the predominant ethnic group of the region, and their influence pervaded the political, economic, and social fabric of southwestern Pennsylvania. Only a few days after easterners heard of the riots at Bower Hill, editorials appeared blaming them on "lawless men, lately arrived from Ireland—a country where oppression reigns and where the people have become habituated to faction." One of the Federalist complaints about the Democratic Societies was that they were "chiefly composed of foreigners." Some immigrants maintained close contact with Ireland. For example, James McFarlane, the rebel leader who would be killed at Bower Hill, not only had a brother in County Tyrone, [Ireland], but had paid the cost of passage to America for John Reed and James Scott. The latter, an indentured servant, immediately ran away at the death of his master.(41)

Some of the rebels were prominent members or members in good standing of the Presbyterian church. Always outspoken on their rights and beliefs, these proud individualists were adherents of Calvinistic dissent. The temperance movement had not yet begun, and most of them had no quibbles with drinking. At the same time, they did feel that they had a moral obligation to protest an unfair tax. Speaking of whiskey consumption in his history of the Redstone Presbytery, Rev. Joseph Smith remarked, "Our ministers and elders used it, as well as their people. Yet they were not intemperate. No instance ever occurred, in which either a minister or an elder ever needed to be subjected to the slightest act of discipline, on this account." In addition, the most prominent Presbyterian clergyman west of the Alleghenies, Rev. John McMillan (1752-1833), although opposed to the excise, was also opposed to violence and refused to allow the dissidents to partake of communion. The following lines from his epitaph express the high esteem in which he was held, "His indefatigable zeal in promoting his Masters cause and the best interests of his fellow men have raised a monument to his fame far more imperishable than the stone which bears this inscription."(42)

View of Peters Creek Baptist Church after it had been converted to a house, from a pastel by J. Howard Iams.

Two Baptist ministers, David Philips and John Corbley, were also active in the Rebellion. Philips (1742-1829), who was a captain in a Chester County, Pennsylvania, battalion during the Revolutionary War and a colonel in his local militia, lived on Peters Creek near Finleyville and led his three congregations on the Monongahela and Youghiogheny rivers in religious revivals during 1793-94. Active in the Rebellion, these areas were experiencing economic changes as well. Philips attended both the first and second meeting of excise petitioners at Pittsburgh.(43) Likewise, Corbley's field of work was in economically developed neighborhoods in the Muddy Creek area of southern Washington County, which were also actively involved in the Rebellion. Corbley (1733-1803) was arrested for being "traitorously assembled" at Braddock's Field and for "confederating to raise an insurrection," and was taken to jail at Philadelphia. Both Philips and Corbley were active in their ministries until they died. Highly visible and vocal men such as Philips and Corbley were seen by the Federalist government as threats to the order of the new nation.(44)

Some members of the Methodist clergy sought to contradict the assertions that they were instigating the Rebellion, and following Washington's admonition, tried to instill in their congregations the need for a peaceful compliance with the excise law. However, the general opposition to the law prevented the preachers' open acceptance of it. In addition, there was much religious rivalry in the 1790s as debates occurred between Methodists and Presbyterians and Methodists and Baptists, as the Methodists tried to gain a foothold in this region which had been previously settled by the Presbyterians and Baptists. The Forks Meetinghouse, later known as Fells Church, was the earliest Methodist Society in Westmoreland County and was centered in the excise protest region.(45)

Germans of different denominations and sects were involved in the protests as well. In addition to the Scotch-Irish, the Germans were perceived as a group of foreigners whose loyalty to democratic ideals was questionable. Like the Scotch-Irish, they too had settled on the frontiers of Pennsylvania because the best eastern lands were already occupied. Noted centers of German unrest were located in and around Bedford, in the Berlin area of Somerset County, in the German Township area of Fayette County, and in Hempfield Township, Westmoreland County.

Herman [Hormon] Husband (1724-1795), perhaps the most influential religious personage of the rebellion, came to the area which became Somerset County after being outlawed in North Carolina for his role in the War of the Regulation in 1771-72. Husband, the Thomas Paine of the Whiskey Rebellion, had the ability to convert his religious zeal and political expectations into inspiring and motivating pamphlets. Widely known as a religious fanatic and called a lunatic by others, he styled himself a prophet of the New Jerusalem. The westerner's role in this millennium was the removal of the tyrannical Federalist government, which conspired to cheat the people of their rights gained during the Revolution. He envisioned a "Glorious Land of Liberty in the Western Country." Husband taught that the "perfect government" is easily accessible to the people, but also that the common people must keep themselves informed of governmental operations, and stand ready to risk their lives and property for freedom. Through his pamphlets he was able to synthesize the western tradition of rebelliousness and the promise of change or revolution with the expectation of a more perfect world in the yet thinly populated spaces of the west. As with the War of the Regulation, he was able to frame the cultural and economic differences between East and West in terms easily understood by the frontiersman. Among the first men arrested by federal troops, he was released from jail in the spring of 1795 but died before he could return home.(46)

As society on the frontier became structured, three key groups emerged to provide a focus of authority. These were the economic, political, and military leaders who tried to direct the course of the whiskey excise protest. Naturally, the distiller was a key element in the movement. Many were members of the economic, political or social elite of their communities. The excise tax profoundly affected them, and the way in which the distiller responded to the tax influenced the community's response. Just as the location of Scotch-Irish settlements would be a determinant of where protests would break out, the reaction of distillers was a principal factor in the Rebellion. The political elites of the region who met at Pittsburgh in September 1791 and August 1792 were composed largely of elected or appointed officials. As such, they were keenly aware that their careers could be built or destroyed by a popular movement with the potential of the excise movement. These men employed the current legal and sometimes extralegal channels to protest the tax. Just as the distillers were a key group in the Rebellion, so also, the public officials of southwestern Pennsylvania were major factors.(47)

The third primary group was the military or militia groups in the region. Militiamen, who had the means for reprimanding excise collectors and their supporters, took encouragement from the actions of western political leaders and the delinquency of distillers there. The most democratic electoral event in the western country, the annual militia muster, was the political arena of the ordinary man. About one-third of the rebels who can be traced through historic records held a militia office or served in a special capacity within a militia unit.(48)

Another group, which is sometimes overlooked, but which nevertheless played a dramatic role in the Whiskey Rebellion is the landless, propertyless, poor inhabitants of the region. They were part of the faceless crowds who attacked excise collectors and their supporters, participated in the Braddock's Field muster, and disrupted the election for submission. In his history of the Rebellion, Brackenridge cautioned his readers, "It is a great mistake to suppose that Bradford or Marshall or others led the people. It was the mass of the people that commanded." These were the people who believed they had a right to protest or even revolt when they were unjustly treated by their government. What some historians term the "moral economy of the crowd" directed that the region's political leaders seek and achieve a public good.(49)

A nineteenth-century print titled, "Tarring and Feathering an Excise Officer."

The Rebellion would pit the friends of liberty, some of whom would be dubbed the "Whiskey Boys," against the friends of order, the Federalist government and their "watermelon army." (The term watermelon army first appeared in a satirical attack on Federalist supporters in *The Pittsburgh Gazette* in which Captain Whiskey declared, "Brothers, you must not think to frighten us with fine arranged lists of infantry, cavalry and artillery, composed of your watermellon armies from the Jersey shores.")(50) The friends of liberty felt the principal task of government was to protect the liberties of the people while the friends of order feared that any questioning or opposition to government might lead to anarchy.

Dissent during the Rebellion took two forms: one, in extralegal meetings which produced resolutions against the excise, and two, in ritualized community censure which resulted in chastisement or violence to the individual or his property. (Extralegal means that the proceedings were not regulated by law: they were not sanctioned by the government in power, but neither could they be determined by this government to be illegal.) The national government failed to differentiate between the two. Although long used by English crowds without formal access to power, the right of political dissent in the form of extralegal association and the custom of blacking had its Pennsylvania origins in Cumberland County in 1765. (The anonymous blacked faces of the participants emphasized that their behavior represented the community's disapproval of the victim's actions.) At that time James Smith and his "Black Boys" tried to stop trade between Philadelphia merchants and western Indians. When entreaties with government officials failed, Smith and his men, who blacked themselves, waylaid the packhorse train at Sideling Hill and destroyed the weapons and trade goods. (51)

A Setting for Rebellion

Synopsis of Events Leading Up to the Rebellion

On March 3, 1791, Congress passed the excise tax. Passage was successful because of a deal struck between northern interests which sought assumption of state debts and southern interests which sought to have the national capital on the Potomac. The legislature of Pennsylvania had voted against the bill's passage prior to its last vote in Congress. Likewise, the legislatures of Maryland, Virginia, North Carolina, and Georgia proclaimed their opposition to the tax as well. The bill detailed in sixty-two sections how each state was to be divided into surveys and districts with supervisors and inspectors. The liquor casks were to be branded and gauged before being removed from the distillery site, and each distiller was to print his occupation, "Distiller of Spirits," on the outside of his distillery. Supervisors were to inspect the still houses. Each distiller was to keep a record of the kinds and quantity of spirits distilled. The president was authorized to make allowances to supervisors for their services out of the product of the duties. No wonder it was termed a "hateful tax!" Pennsylvania Senator William Maclay, suspicious of Hamilton's motives, feared the result of the tax would be "war and bloodshed."(52)

The first extralegal excise meeting took place on July 27, 1791, when a small group of politicians from the region met at Redstone Old Fort (Brownsville). They resolved to send representatives to another meeting at Pittsburgh and draft petitions to Congress for repeal of the excise law. On September 6, Robert Johnson became the first excise officer to experience an attack. However, the participants were described as dressed in women's clothes rather than having blackened faces, another traditional crowd practice. The politically prominent Hamiltons of Mingo Creek were among those charged in this offense. The meeting at Pittsburgh occurred the day after the attack on collector Johnson. Later that fall a crowd carrying tar and feathers surrounded Benjamin Wells's excise office in Greensburg, which he had just opened.(53)

In March 1792 Secretary of the Treasury Alexander Hamilton reported to Congress on the problems of enforcing the excise law. As a result Congress, in May of that year, modified the excise law to reduce the rates and to allow for monthly payments. This did not satisfy the opposition to the tax. In August, twenty men dressed as Indians ransacked the tavern/house of Captain William Faulkner in Washington town. Faulkner had offered to let his building be used as an excise office, but soon revoked his offer after threats of violence continued. Depositions in the Faulkner court case indicated an "association" of up to five hundred men had been formed at Mingo Creek to oppose the excise law.(54)

That same August representatives from Fayette, Allegheny, and Washington counties assembled at Tannehill's tavern in Pittsburgh to seek legal measures to repeal the excise law. In addition, they requested that their fellow citizens join them in ostracizing those who had accepted excise offices or complied with the excise. Most national government leaders, particularly Hamilton and Washington, objected to this type of meeting. However, Attorney General Edmund Randolph concluded that no laws had been broken and that "to assemble and remonstrate to the legislature are among the rights of citizens." President Washington, fearing that these meetings constituted a threat to order and following Hamilton's advice of a martial tone, issued a proclamation in September 1792 to desist from all unlawful proceedings. He warned that his administration would treat unkindly any attempt to obstruct the laws of the United States, in particular the excise law.(55)

As a result of Washington's action, the moderate faction, those opposed to the excise but who did not advocate violence, called no further meetings for almost two years—or until after the actual Rebellion had broken out. Thus, the Washington administration had effectively eliminated a safety valve. Through Federalist writings in the press, the Pittsburgh meeting was given the appearance of an illegal opposition. This served to make the excise tax more popular in the East and defeated the cause of the protesters. Although the moderates did not become actively involved again until the Rebellion had begun, other elected officials, such as David Bradford, representing the radical faction, took advantage of the situation.(56)

The events of August and September 1792 foreshadowed the clash that would occur two years later. Both sides were adamant on the excise tax question. George Washington (1732-1799) understood it to be his duty to come out of retirement and to serve his country as president. He also saw that it was his duty "to carry the Laws of the United States into effect." Washington took personally any opposition to the nation's laws as opposition to him as well. He felt the excise law was a just law, and he concluded that protesting the excise law equalled a general opposition to government. He also perceived that the opposition to the excise law in western Pennsylvania was equivalent to advocating separation from the union, "the most dreadful of all calamities."(57)

In May of 1792 Congress passed an act to more effectively provide for the national defense by establishing a uniform militia throughout the United States. It stated that "every free able-bodied male citizen of the respective states of the age of eighteen years and under the age of forty-five shall be enrolled in the militia by the commanding officer of the company within whose bounds such citizen shall reside." The simple fact that common men were armed and organized militarily contributed greatly to the ease with which the excise opposition moved toward rebellion. Accounts showed that musters were important occasions for organizing opposition to the tax. As previously mentioned, militiamen were the third group of people with a major impact on the Rebellion. Many of the officers in the militias had served in the Revolutionary War and believed that many of the issues at stake in the Whiskey Rebellion were those they had fought for previously. Militiamen had the means, the arms, and the traditional precedents for censuring excisemen and for taking extralegal measures.(58)

J. Howard Iams's wood block print of a "Burning Cabin."

Treasury Secretary Alexander Hamilton sent Pennsylvania Supervisor of Collection George Clymer to Pittsburgh in September to seek information about anti-excise activities in the western country. (Clymer, 1739-1813, a signer of the Declaration of Independence, was a wealthy Philadelphia merchant and land speculator. His son would join the federal army to suppress the rebels and die of lockjaw while in western Pennsylvania.) Clymer's letter to Hamilton concerning his mission reinforced Hamilton's notion that the political and religious leaders of the region were instigating the acts of violence. In December 1792 three Methodist circuit riders of western Pennsylvania wrote to Washington disavowing the assertions made by Clymer. In particular, Clymer portrayed antifederalist politicians William Findley (1750-1821) and John Smilie (1741-1813) as having corrupted and disaffected the masses.(59) (State Senator Smilie attended the August 1792 Pittsburgh meeting. Although there is no other record of his participation in the excise protest, Hamilton names him as among the officials who influenced the participation of the masses in the protest.) In October Clymer reported to the federal court held in York the names of those involved in the protests. It was the opinion of Attorney General Edmund Randolph, however, that the proceedings at Pittsburgh were not an indictable offense.(60)

Undoubtedly the key player on the Federalist side of the excise issue was Alexander Hamilton (1756-1804). Washington recognized Hamilton's writing skills as pamphleteer during the early days of the Revolution and made him a secretary and later an aide-de-camp. He soon became Washington's trusted advisor. Nearly from the beginning, he was a proponent of a highly centralized authority. Appointed secretary of the treasury in 1789, Hamilton soon had a scheme for funding the national debt. An excise on spirits would put the country in the black. It was Hamilton who in September 1792 advised Washington that "if the processes of the Courts are resisted, to employ those means, which in the last resort are put in the power of the Executive."(61) However, Washington emphasized in his response that "Regular Troops" were to be employed only as a last recourse. Westmoreland County Congressman William Findley immediately recognized Hamilton's scheme to make western Pennsylvanians examples and advised that their actions be taken with guarded moderation.(62) Although the tax could neither be collected in the frontier areas of the Carolinas, Virginia, or Kentucky, the potential success of armed suppression in these areas was not as assured as in Pennsylvania. Hamilton also played a chief role in the quelling of the Rebellion, acting as superintending official of General Henry Lee's punitive force.

In October 1792 Philip Wigle (Vigol), son of a Westmoreland County miller, denounced and beat excise collector Benjamin Wells at his father's mill. In April of the following year eight men with blackened faces attacked Wells's office at Connellsville. Wells, excise collector for Fayette County, was notoriously unpopular. This arose from the fact that he had not only harassed distillers but had also informed on those who would not register. Wells was not only persistent in collecting the excise but also in submitting claims to the national government for losses suffered during rebel attacks.(63)

Sporadic excise protests continued throughout the remainder of 1793. In June of that year Washington County militia burned "General Neville the excise man" in effigy during a militia officer election held at the forks of the Youghiogheny and Monongahela rivers. In November, Wells's house was broken into again. After the break-in, Wells promised to print his resignation in *The Pittsburgh Gazette*. Robert Smilie, John McCulloch, and four others were charged with being riotous with "sticks, staves and clubs" during this incident. (Smilie was a son of John Smilie, antifederalist congressman of Fayette County.) Although there were as many violent acts in 1793 as in the previous two years, both Secretary Hamilton and antifederalist politician Albert Gallatin presumed that the excise law had gained ground that year. One reason they so believed may have been that they were cut off from the people as a consequence of Washington's ban on extralegal meetings. Again, the year 1793 saw no excise revenues entering federal coffers from any frontier region.(64)

While protests continued beyond the Alleghenies, the operations of the national government in Philadelphia came to a virtual standstill as the yellow fever epidemic spread throughout the city. The epidemic, along with conflicts in Europe, prevented the Washington administration from acting on the excise protest. Western protesters interpreted this inaction as a lack of resolve on the part of the government, and this encouraged their perseverance in seeking repeal.

The radical faction of protesters began 1794 in full force. This group burned the barns of William Richmond and Robert Shawhan in St. Clair Township, Allegheny County, for their compliance with the excise law. This marked a turning point in the protest in that violence no longer was committed only against collectors or collection houses, but was also against those who appeared to be in league with the collectors. (The rebels generally targeted commercial properties such as mills or stills.) In February 1794 Supervisor Neville reported that "persons living near the line of Allegheny and Washington counties made threats that they would not leave a house standing in Allegheny County owned by a person complying with the law."(65)

Meanwhile back east during February, President Washington issued a proclamation calling on authorities to discover and bring to justice those who had assaulted excise collector Benjamin Wells in November. In addition, the United States House of Representatives established a committee to learn what legislative measures might be necessary to collect the duties on domestically distilled spirits. Their study resulted in a congressional amendment to the excise law in June which enabled trials of tax evaders in local state courts. In a further concession, small distillers were allowed a license for stills which were to operate for less than a year. This bill also made it easier for Supervisor Neville, who no longer needed to establish offices in each of the four counties but could operate from a central office in Pittsburgh.

On February 28, 1794, the constitution of what many leaders in the national government termed the "Mingo Creek Democratic Society" was approved. (Many later historians have followed the Federalist interpretation and designated this organization a democratic society.) However, the group referred to themselves in this document as the "society of united freemen of Hamilton's district of Washington County." This district took its name from its polling place, the home of David Hamilton. The Hamilton's district society may have been its more appropriate name, since this group was unlike the true democratic-republican associations founded in Philadelphia in 1793-94 as part of the enthusiastic response to the French Revolution.(66) The Hamilton's district or Mingo Creek group was an association similar to the political committees of correspondence established throughout the American colonies during the Revolution. In all probability, the origins of the Mingo group can be traced to at least 1792 when an "association" is recorded as having instigated the attack on Faulkner's tavern. Both Hugh Brackenridge and William Findley, in their writings following the Rebellion, noted the Mingo Creek region as the "cradle" or "seat" of the insurrection.(67) The Mingo society or association was organized through their militia regiment. The leaders or representatives of the eight companies within the regiment represented the individual members on a council which met on a monthly basis. The society's secretary, John McDonald, said that moderate members of the group sought to use it as a forum to prevent further violence by excise resisters.

J. Howard Iams's c. 1936 rendition of a tar and feathering.

A month after the Mingo society was formally established, the constitution of the Washington Democratic Society was signed by thirty-two prominent Washington County residents. This society was more like the clubs established in Philadelphia to discuss political subjects. However, since some of its members, such as David Bradford, John Canon, and James Marshall, were also involved in excise protest meetings, President Washington scorned these "self-created" societies as fomenters of instability. A similar society was founded in Allegheny County in April.(68)

Generally, the members of these societies were newcomers to the political field who resolved to transform the process of political decision making. They saw themselves as imitating the revolutionary societies of the American Revolution and sought ways to articulate representative democracy in the face of established political forces. Although these societies contributed to the birth of the Republican and Federalist parties, they never recovered from the Federalist claim that they precipitated the Whiskey Rebellion.(69)

A letter from George Clymer to excise collector Robert Johnson in March 1794 indicates the federal government was planning its move against the people of western Pennsylvania. Clymer wrote that the excise collectors of the Fourth Survey should come to Philadelphia and make a full report on any persons in civil or military employment of either the state or federal government "who have in any respect infringed the laws or unlawfully impeded or prevented their execution by violence, menaces, holding unentered stills, etc." They were likewise to report on any private persons who had done any of the same things.(70)

At the end of May, District Attorney William Rawle, not waiting for the pending law in Congress which would allow trials in local courts, secured processes from the federal court in Philadelphia. These processes ordered the appearance of sixty western distillers before the court in Philadelphia during August. More than three weeks later and after the excise bill had been amended, U.S. Marshal David Lennox began his journey west to deliver these processes.

As already mentioned, the excise law was amended on June 5. On that same day the "Revenue Act of 1794" passed both houses of Congress. This new excise law placed levies on snuff manufactured for sale and sugar refined in the United States. As excise protesters had predicted, an excise tax on whiskey would lead to a multitude of indirect taxes. These new taxes broadened support for the developing Democratic-Republican party.(71)

In June of 1794 radical protest intensified. Acts of violence were centered in southern Allegheny and northern Washington counties. James Kiddoe of Mifflin Township, Allegheny County, who had earlier had his barn burned, now had parts of his gristmill carried away because he adhered to the excise law. About the same time, John Lynn, deputy excise collector for Washington County, was tarred and feathered. His house in Canonsburg was attacked a few days later and partly torn down. William Cochran, also of Mifflin Township, Allegheny County, received an additional assessment for his compliance with the excise. In two separate attacks by insurgents, his large still, with a capacity of 120 gallons, was wrecked, the "superfine boulting cloth" from his flour mill was destroyed, and "sundry irons" were taken from his sawmill. It would be another month before his distillery was back in production.(72)

Action!

Open Rebellion Begins

The crisis of the so-called Whiskey Rebellion, transpiring all along the western frontier, reached a climax in late July and early August of 1794 in the four western counties of Pennsylvania: Fayette, Westmoreland, Allegheny, and Washington. Violence erupted on July 15 when U.S. Marshal David Lennox delivered a court summons to farmer/distiller William Miller in Allegheny County and brought with him the despised Supervisor of Collection, John Neville. (Lennox had completed his rounds in Cumberland, Bedford, and Fayette counties without incident.) The first summons of the day had been delivered to Colonel David Philips, who was in his field harvesting. Preacher/militia leader Philips, immediately began calling on and collecting his neighbors. Menacingly following the marshal and Neville, they acted the role of a posse. Although the group whooped and hallooed and a gun was fired, no further violence occurred that day. These Allegheny County farmer/distillers believed that the marshal was dragging men off to jail in Philadelphia. Consequently, they thought another right was being taken from them—that of a trial in their vicinage. This right became the number-one issue when representatives met at Parkinson's Ferry in the middle of August. The excise tax was not mentioned until the second resolution of that meeting.(73)

The next morning a group of about forty men, about half of whom were armed, visited Neville's house and demanded his resignation and all records associated with the tax. Neville, however, refused and opened fire on the rebels. Fearing trouble, Neville had earlier armed his slaves. They fired on the rebels from the rear. Five of the rebels fell wounded, and one of them, Oliver Miller, possibly a nephew to William, died later that day. The defeated rebels returned to Couch's Fort where they planned their next move.(74)

Neville (1731-1803) was the government's key contact in the West. A native of Virginia, he served with distinction in the Revolution. After the war he settled in Pennsylvania, where he became a large landholder and distiller. In 1791 Washington appointed him Inspector of Revenue for the western counties. Previously he had opposed the excise tax, so his ready acceptance gave the perception that he had received a bribe to do so. Until that time he had been a popular and honored figure in the West. Neville played a pivotal role in the Rebellion, not only as a conduit of information to the federal government in Philadelphia, but also in his resolve to keep the excise offices open. His refusal to resign his commission as requested by the rebels not only resulted in the deaths of several insurgents and the burning of his mansion, but set the stage for a large-scale insurrection. Had he relinquished his commission as other excise collectors had, the insurrection might never have started. Neville's son-in-law Isaac Craig was deputy quartermaster general for the army and as such controlled who sold whiskey to the army, the largest consumer of

A block print of "Counsel Before the Attack at General Neville's House," portraying negotiations between the troops from Ft. Fayette and the militiamen under Captain James McFarlane.

spirits in the West. Intimately connected with the military and political powers of the Federalist government, Neville became a favored, large whiskey producer who was helping to push the small producer out. He was among the small, influential group in western Pennsylvania who stubbornly supported the excise, and distinguished the region from other frontier areas where no group adhered to the law.(75)

The day following the first march on the Neville house, an organized band of locals, about six hundred strong, headed by local Revolutionary hero James McFarlane, returned to the scene. (Between confrontations, Neville had secured the help of his brother-in-law Major Abraham Kirkpatrick and ten soldiers from Fort Fayette at Pittsburgh.) The surrender of Neville and his resignation as excise officer was requested by the group. The offer was declined as Neville had been secreted in a nearby ravine. After the exchange of messages between the groups, who allowed the remaining Neville family to evacuate, firing began on both sides. During a lull in the fighting, McFarlane thought he heard a call for a parley. He stepped from behind a tree and was immediately shot and killed. McFarlane (1751-1794) became the best-known martyr of the rebel cause. An officer of the Revolution and council member of the Mingo Creek Society, he had been selected to lead the militias on the march to the Neville house. A large group of friends and relatives buried him at Mingo Creek Presbyterian Churchyard in the heart of the excise protest region. Captain James McFarlane's grave was dressed, and a tombstone placed on it in 1798. This large, flat tombstone, including its cutting and hauling from Pittsburgh, cost about the price of 150 gallons of whiskey—a pretty penny for the canonization of a Whiskey Rebellion hero. Its inscription tells much about the time and its people:

> He served throughout the war with undaunted courage in the defense of American Independence against the lawless and despotic encroachments of Great Britain. He fell at last by the hands of an unprincipled villain in support of what he supposed to be the rights of his country...(76)

(The rank of captain was bestowed during his service in the Rebellion. He had attained the rank of major during the Revolution.)

McFarlane's death temporarily stunned and confused the militia, but they continued shooting while others set fire to Neville's barn and outbuildings. The conflagration consumed everything except a few slave quarters. The mansion was burned last, one of the most finely appointed houses in the west. (Accused insurrectionist Alexander Fulton stated in his petition to Washington that he saved Neville's "meal house and the provisions in it.") Several men were wounded on both sides during the melee, and one of the soldiers from Fort Fayette died as well.(77)

A few days after the Bower Hill incidents, John Reed, a prominent distiller of Mifflin Township, Allegheny County, was warned by "Tom the Tinker" to attend gatherings such as those at Neville's or be "deemed an enemy of republican liberty." This marked the first known use of the term "Tom the Tinker" in association with

View of Mingo Creek Churchyard showing the large tablet in left foreground which memorializes James McFarlane.

the militant faction of rebels. The term has been credited to John Holcroft, who was one of the leaders of this faction of rebels. Since the shooting-up of stills came to be known as "mending the still," and a tinker was an itinerant peddler who mended pots and pans, the name seemed appropriate. A native of Connecticut and previously involved in Shays' Rebellion, Holcroft (1741-1816) was living in the Mingo Creek area of Washington County by the 1780s. A militia leader, Holcroft led the band of rebels during the first confrontation at Neville's house. The Tom the Tinker signature, placed on broadsides and in newspaper advertisements warning people not to cooperate with the excise law, became known statewide.(78)

Following the riots at Bower Hill, State Representative Albert Gallatin helped to keep Fayette County from becoming further involved in acts of violence. He attended an excise meeting in Uniontown on July 20. The distillers present agreed to obey the law by either registering their stills at the excise office or abandoning them.

On July 23 a meeting was held at Mingo Creek Presbyterian Meetinghouse to determine what direction the western country should take after the events at Bower Hill the week previous. David Bradford (c.1760-c.1807), deputy attorney general for Washington County and vice-president of the Washington Democratic Society, defended the actions of the rebels at Bower Hill and became leader of the radical faction of rebels throughout the remainder of the insurrection. A rising lawyer and landholder in Washington, Bradford masterminded the interception of the mail from Pittsburgh to Philadelphia. He used some of the stolen letters from Federalist sympathizers in Pittsburgh, which condemned the riot, as a justification to call a regional militia muster at Braddock's Field. The Braddock's Field rendezvous signified the translation of words to action. Here, Bradford was elected major general to command the militia forces. Bradford's name was at the top of the list of those to be arrested by the federal troops. However, he fled to Louisiana, never again to take up residence in Pennsylvania or regain a prominent position politically. (Bradford died near present-day St. Francisville, Louisiana.) He had the distinction of being the only rebel Washington never pardoned.(79)

About a week after the Neville incident, the excise office of John Wells was attacked. Wells, a son of the infamous Benjamin, had opened an excise office in Philip Reagan's house in East Huntingdon Township, Westmoreland County, only a month or so previous. During the attack, Reagan's new barn and its contents were destroyed along with some of his crops in the field.(80) In conjunction with this attack, rebels burned the excise office of Benjamin Wells at Connellsville after he failed to heed their warnings to close it. The previous March some of the more prominent distillers and political leaders of Fayette County had proposed registering their stills if the detestable Wells were removed from office and replaced with an honest and respectable man. Philip Wigle, one of those charged in this attack, would be one of those rounded up by the army and taken to Philadelphia to stand trial. He was found guilty of high treason. Albert Gallatin described him as a rough, ignorant German, who was an object of pity. Gallatin alleged that although Wigle knew he was

27

Print of John Holcroft, alias Tom the Tinker, from the original painting by Charles Reader.

committing a riot, he did not understand that it amounted to levying war and high treason.(81)

John Webster, tavernkeeper and excise collector for Bedford County, suffered the wrath of the rebels next. Webster's letters to Neville portray an opportunistic man who was not above using his office for economic gain. He had his home and office at Stoney Creek in Quemahoning Township (now Somerset County just southeast of Stoystown) during the Rebellion. About 150 men from Westmoreland County threatened him with tar and feathers, demanded his commission, and made him promise never to collect the excise again. A submissive Webster was marched west for a few miles where he was ordered to mount a stump, recant his promises not to act as collector again, and hurrah three times for Tom the Tinker. Although his house was not touched, his stable and hay stacks were burned.(82)

The zenith of the Rebellion was reached in early August during the military rally called at Braddock's Field. Contemporary sources estimated that between five and seven thousand armed militiamen responded to the call, more than half the taxable males of the western counties. Rebel leaders conceived the rally as a power play, not only to show the strength of anti-excise feeling in the region to Federalists in Pittsburgh and Philadelphia, but also to coerce additional support from local farmer/distillers. Although they marched on Pittsburgh, extensive violence was prevented through the efforts of men such as Hugh Brackenridge. In addition the townspeople of Pittsburgh proved hospitable to the rebels, providing them with casks of whiskey. Included in the terms of negotiations to save Pittsburgh from destruction was the banning of certain obnoxious persons (basically Federalist sympathizers known from opening the mail).

Since Major Kirkpatrick was reportedly responsible for McFarlane's death, it was generally thought that his Pittsburgh property was in danger of destruction. McFarlane's brother Andrew and Colonel Edward Cook were among those who prevented a few of the radicals from burning the house. However, they were unable to prevent the burning of his barn on the opposite side of the Monongahela. Cook and other prominent men, mostly from Washington County, disavowed this burning and reimbursed Kirkpatrick's tenant for the damages done.(83)

Although the militia were said to have marched the eight miles from Braddock's field to Pittsburgh in good order, newspaper advertisements indicate that the order was far from perfect. Two weeks later, Jonathan Coulter, Captain, near Devore's Ferry, Washington County, sought a rifle "lifted on the parade at Pittsburgh." Another advertisement about a month later stated, "George Robinson found an English musket while on the march from Braddock's Field to this Place."(84)

The man with perhaps the single most political influence in Allegheny County at the time of the Rebellion was Hugh Henry Brackenridge. Lawyer and satirical writer, Brackenridge (1748-1816) acted as a mediating force during the Rebellion. Although he appears to be duplicitous at times, he actually sought what was best for the western country. However, his efforts at temporizing the situation at Braddock's Field perhaps gave the militant excise resistance a false sense of legitimacy, which may have prolonged opposition. Brackenridge served the important and dangerous role of intermediary between government authorities and protesters of the excise. He learned that he couldn't please either side and was suspected and hated on the extremes of both sides. To use his own words, he "shewed a readiness to sacrifice popular favour for the public good." He was in danger of losing his life as a traitor to the friends of liberty or being charged with treason by the federal government. As an active participant in a democratic society he was naturally offended by the allegations of insurrectionary intentions by the government he was supporting. Controversial throughout his public career, he tried to vindicate his role in the Rebellion with his detailed account, *Incidents of the Insurrection in the Western Parts of Pennsylvania in the year 1794*, printed in 1795.(85)

Washington's cabinet met the same day as the march on Pittsburgh to discuss the events in the western counties of Pennsylvania. Discussion centered on whether or not to call out the militia to restore peace. Federal law required that a Supreme Court justice declare that a state of rebellion existed in order for the president to issue an order for troops. Pennsylvania Supreme Court Justice and architect of the United States Constitution James Wilson, who favored a strong centralized government over state sovereignty, fulfilled this necessity on August 4. In the meantime, Pennsylvania Governor Thomas Mifflin pleaded with Washington that the military power of the government ought not to be employed until its judicial authority has been proven incapable of enforcing obedience. Mifflin's labors had a limited success. In the first weeks of August, the Washington administration sought a peaceful solution to the crisis in exchange for Mifflin's cooperation in raising troops within the state. Mifflin feared that a military force brought into the region would also alienate the peaceable citizens of the region and cause more discontent there.(86)

When it was learned by the middle of September that certain county militia groups were not willing to send forces against their own countrymen, Mifflin effectively appealed to their patriotism. Those who served in the county militias during this campaign were given a bounty, but those who would not serve and didn't find a replacement for their service, were fined. A Revolutionary War officer, and Pennsylvania's governor since 1790, Mifflin (1744-1800) appears to have been caught between what he believed were state judicial rights and Hamilton's quest for central control. His efforts were no match for Hamilton's thrust for power. Consequently, states' rights finished second in this contest.(87)

After pondering the issue for a few days, Washington issued a proclamation on August 7 detailing his interpretation of events on the frontier since 1791. Western political leaders were blamed for fomenting unrest among "the ignorant poor." He informed the nation of his preliminary efforts to raise troops, and ordered the insurgents "to disperse and retire peaceably to their respective abodes" by September First. Secretary of State Edmund Randolph persuaded the President to send a peace commission to theWest, and the following day Washing-

A pre-1920 view of the two-bay, frame and stone Andrew McFarlane house which overlooked the Monongahela River at Elrama, near the border of Allegheny and Washington counties.

ton dispatched a delegation consisting of Attorney General William Bradford, Pennsylvania Supreme Court Justice Jasper Yeates, and Senator James Ross of Washington County to mediate an end to the rebellion. Governor Mifflin had appointed Chief Justice Thomas McKean and General William Irvine to act as peace commissioners for Pennsylvania two days previous.(88)

Unrest continued west of the Alleghenies and spread east of the mountains by the middle of the month. Liberty poles appeared for the first time in Brownsville, Greensburg, Uniontown, and Washington town, among other places. Not only did the liberty pole serve as an emblem of rebel unrest, it also provided a rallying point for discussions on the political questions and controversies of 1794. The national government was very sensitive to its symbolism. Many of the charges of treason associated with the Whiskey Rebellion stemmed from erecting liberty poles or attending a gathering at a liberty pole. (A symbol against tyranny, this pole, usually of spliced timbers, could be bound with iron rings or studded with nails. It could elevate an official flag or banner, or a home-made version, most often inscribed with the words "Equal Taxation and No Excise" or "Liberty and Equality.") In mid-August, citizens of Cumberland County met at Newville to petition the government for repeal of the excise tax, as well as to plan for another meeting at Carlisle at the end of the month. In Hagerstown, Maryland, an advertisement, written in German, was posted on the markethouse, charging certain Federalists with cutting down the liberty pole which excise protesters had erected there.(89)

Silhouette of Hugh H. Brackenridge, taken from a drawing by Robert Smith.

The news of what was happening in the West spread eastward by word of mouth, by letter, or by broadside, and bits of information were eventually printed in the newspapers. It would have been hard to detect a national crisis from reading any of the newspapers across the state. Often the rumors printed helped to heighten the misunderstandings between East and West, between Federalist and Republican. It took two weeks for the information of the riots at Bower Hill to be printed in the *Gazette of the United States and Daily Evening Advertiser,* a Philadelphia newspaper printed by John Fenno, an ardent backer of the Federalist cause. The news of Bower Hill had been printed six days earlier by another Philadelphia paper, the *General Advertiser.* Its editor Benjamin Franklin Bache was privy only to fragmentary reports, which contributed to his vacillations in reporting the western peace progress. Although Bache passionately backed the Republican cause, his editorials were the only ones to perceive that not only were the rebels to blame for the riots, but the central government as well. In response to Hamilton's first "Tully" letter, Bache wrote:

> *Every man must be sensible of the errors and offences committed by our western brethren, but let us not abandon the endeavor to reclaim and reform them, by reason and good offices, in compliment to the passions of an irascible politician, or to the dexterity of a skillful penman.*

Helping to build the animosity toward westerners, the Hamilton-backed Fenno paper wrote on August 20:

> *By some recent accounts from the westward, we learn that the views of the Insurgents in that quarter are more extensively*

> *hostile to the peace, unity and indivisibility of the United States than has been generally supposed...The opposition to the Excise on Whisky is but an ostensible business to cover the commencement of a more extensive plan...& that is an excission [sic] of the Counties over the Mountains from the Union.*

Perhaps ironically, both editors died as a result of the yellow fever epidemic of 1793. (90)

Whereas the Philadelphia papers were very much directed to foreign intelligence and maritime travel, *Kline's Carlisle Weekly Gazette* filled its news columns with local and current news from Pittsburgh and Philadelphia. Until 1793 the paper had been titled, *The Carlisle Gazette and Western Repository of Knowledge*, and it appears to have been more efficient in reporting news from the West, including Hagerstown, Fredericktown, Pittsburgh, and Kentucky. Edited by German immigrant and political activist George Kline, its reporting appears more evenhanded, and more letters from the general populace appear on its pages, than the eastern papers of the period. An item dated August 30 from Pittsburgh was printed in the September Third issue of the paper. It read in part,

> *We are happy in hearing from various parts of the country that the people are heartily disposed to adopt the terms of accommodation offered on the part of the Commissioners...and that we shall soon have an end of the disorders which threatened the peace and tranquillity of this flourishing part of the United States.(91)*

However true this information may have been, Federalist supporters helped spread contradictory intelligence to insure that troops would be marched against the West. After trials of the rebels began, Kline was subpoenaed to appear in federal court with copies of his newspapers from July through September 1794.

Possibly due to threats to its editor, *The Pittsburgh Gazette* had more complete coverage of the charges and countercharges, political turmoil, and rampant fears within the region. Still, pioneer frontier editor John Scull (1765-1828) was reserved in his coverage, and only after the army had arrived in the West did he completely reveal his Federalist leanings. Unlike the Philadelphia papers, the Pittsburgh and Carlisle papers occasionally placed news of the Rebellion on their front page.(92)

Elected representatives (226 delegates in all) from each township of Pennsylvania's four western counties, plus two representatives from Bedford County, and three from Ohio County, Virginia, met at Parkinson's Ferry on August 14. The meeting took place on the shoulder of a hill overlooking the Monongahela River. (This spot would become known as Whiskey Point.) Albert Gallatin, representative in the Pennsylvania Assembly, opposed David Bradford's radical proposal to obtain arms and raise an army for protection against eastern forces. Gallatin's speech opened the door for an alternate solution to the crisis, one that would enable peace to be restored in the western country. This meeting was instrumental in breaking the power of the radical insurrectionary faction.(93) One of the actions that came out of the Parkinson's Ferry meeting was the resolution to protect the persons and property of individuals. The peace faction had

Illustration of a liberty pole.

found a voice and energetic leadership in Gallatin, who checked and outmaneuvered Bradford. Although the Federalists would later charge that the Parkinson's Ferry meeting was indicative of an insurrection in the western counties, Gallatin countered that not to have had a public forum where private citizens and public officials and the various factions could discuss the situation would only have exacerbated the situation. It provided an opportunity for men like Gallatin to try to dissuade the offenders from further acts of violence, or risk the event of a general rebellion. It was also here that western people first became aware of the President's August 7 proclamation, and they were generally angered by it. The representatives elected a committee to confer with the federal and state commissioners.(94)

Albert Gallatin (1761-1849), representing Fayette County, was a key figure in the extralegal excise meetings. A native Swiss, he was elected to the state legislature in 1790. He penned a series of resolutions, his very first legislative writings, which were introduced into the General Assembly in January 1791. In short, these resolutions strongly criticized the excise as "subversive of the peace, liberty, and rights of the citizen." Passed by a good majority, these were intended to affect the bill before the United States Congress. Of course the Federalist national government considered this meddling, but Hamilton would exact revenge on the state of Pennsylvania later. Gallatin served as clerk of the August 1792 meeting at Pittsburgh to rectify the excise law. This meeting drew the wrath of Washington, who said, "I shall exert all the legal powers with which the executive is invested, to check so daring and unwarrantable spirit."(95) Later in his speech to the Pennsylvania House of Representatives in January 1795, Gallatin admitted his part in this conference as "his only political sin." He further said, "The sentiments thus expressed were not illegal or criminal; yet they were violent, intemperate, and reprehensible. For by attempting to render the office [of excise collector] contemptible, they tended to diminish that respect for the execution of the laws which is essential to the maintenance of a free government." Near the end of his life, when questioned about the content of his speech, he recalled, "I was very modest and did not ascribe to myself all the merit to which I was entitled on that occasion."(96)

Gallatin played a decisive, moderating role in the Rebellion during August and September. He effectively blocked Bradford's proposals at Parkinson's Ferry, and after a speech of some hours at Redstone, he carried the battle for submission to the laws. The Rebellion was essentially broken, but now the westerners had to fear the federal army instead of Tom the Tinker's rioters. Feeling in the army ran high against Gallatin since he had been a prominent leader of opposition to the excise law. John Adams, in writing to Thomas Jefferson in 1813, termed the Rebellion, "Gallatins Insurrection." Unlike Brackenridge, he refused to let considerations of his political future interfere with his responsibilities as a democratic political leader. In addition, Gallatin's stand was representative of Fayette County's moderate stand in not being inclined to join the armed opposition to the law.(97)

Voucher for the cost of warning the militias in Dauphin County to be ready to march against the insurgents in western Pennsylvania.

The Peace Process Begins and the Federal Army Marches West

Three days after the Parkinson's Ferry meeting on August 17, the peace commissioners wrote to Washington that military force would be necessary to quell the insurrection. This was based on information gathered along the way west and from Federalists in Pittsburgh. They had not yet met with the representatives from the four counties, nor had they conferred with the Pennsylvania Commissioners. This information set in motion the military expedition against the rebels. When the letter arrived in Philadelphia (August 23), the Washington administration reversed its policy and began immediate plans for military action. From then on any action or effort for peace by the Commissioners or moderate leaders would be ineffectual.(98)

On August 20 a conference was held at Pittsburgh between the three United States Commissioners, two Pennsylvania Commissioners and the three committeemen from each of the four western counties appointed at Parkinson's Ferry. All of the committee members except Bradford favored submission and the terms offered by the Commissioners. They agreed that the full committee of sixty was to meet with the Commissioners in eight days at Redstone Old Fort (Brownsville).

Fifty-seven of the county representatives showed up at Brownsville. Gallatin, Brackenridge, and Washington County Associate Judge James Edgar spoke for submission to the laws, while Bradford argued for secession and armed resistance. The representatives voted thirty-four to twenty-three for submission. Although this was a victory for the moderates, the United States Commissioners concluded that the size of the negative vote indicated that the laws would not be restored without military coercion. While moderate western leaders saw the results of Redstone positively, the U.S. Commissioners were embittered by the vote there. They were "embarrassed" by the proceedings and sought the vote of individuals on the eleventh to make a "real determination of the Western People and in producing either a sincere submission or such an open resistance as will unite all the friends of the Country against them."(99) This reasoning by the Commissioners was not surprising since two of them had decided on their way west that force would be necessary. Bradford and Yeates felt that the government could not rely on the rebels' submission and expressed this to the government on September 5. When this arrived in Philadelphia September 8, it was the death knell for a negotiated peace.

On August 23 Secretary Hamilton began his pseudonymous "Tully" letters to Philadelphia newspapers with the intent of undermining peace negotiations by asserting that the western riots were part of a concerted plot to overthrow the government. Two days later he wrote to Governor Henry Lee that the militia of Virginia would be used to quell the insurrection. However, the orders for assembling the militia were not to be issued before September 1.(100)

The beginning of September marked an upsurge of activity on the part of the national, state, and local officials and representatives. The United States and Pennsylvania Commissioners and Standing Committee met at Pittsburgh on September 1. It was agreed that a referen-

Lithograph of Albert Gallatin from an original painting by Chappel.

dum would be held on September 11 in the four western counties. Male citizens above the age of eighteen years were required to vote whether they would submit to the laws of the United States.

Also on the first, Governor Richard Howell of New Jersey ordered the troops requested by Washington to rendezvous at Trenton. At the same time, attempts to draft men in the Hagerstown, Maryland, area led to riots. Militiamen "beat their officers from the field," and raised a liberty pole with a flag inscribed with the words "Liberty or Death." Frederick, Maryland, Militia Major-General Mountjoy Bailey quelled the riots with 320 troops, seventy of whom were mounted. One local history states that the riot was confined to "the rabble of the town," and the spirit of the rioters was ephemeral, "inspired by whiskey fresh from the stills."(101)

Meanwhile, Alexander Addison (1759-1807), president judge of the western district, charged the grand jury of Allegheny County to accept the conditions proposed by the United States Commissioners because the cost of war and secession would be devastating to the western region. Like Governor Mifflin, Addison was concerned with state vs. federal powers, particularly judicial powers. He stated that if "the State courts should punish and suppress these riots, the federal courts would have less or no inducement to interfere in them." Copies of Addison's long, wordy directive ran in newspapers across the state. Although Addison was opposed to the excise tax, he felt that it could have been collected if men of principle had been chosen to be collectors. However, the national government ignored Addison's earlier advice.(102)

Despite the fact that the militias were already gathering in the East, commissioners and representatives in the West were still trying to bring peace to the region without the military. The Pennsylvania Commissioners Thomas McKean and William Irvine wrote to Governor Mifflin on September 5 that judicial powers might be sufficient to reduce the rebels to submission without military aid. A few days later a meeting of township representatives was held in Uniontown. As a consequence, Gallatin also wrote to Mifflin advising him not to send troops from other states because of the violence that might result.(103)

On September 9 Secretary Hamilton called for the assembly of Pennsylvania militia, with the general rendezvous to be at Carlisle. Josiah Harmar, adjutant general of the militia of Pennsylvania, gave the orders for each county's militia. The orders specified the quotas for each county and the place where the men were to assemble. Counties from Philadelphia to as far west as Huntingdon were included in the orders. The initial county returns in late August and early September in response to the militia quota requests were generally negative. However, after the eastern counties learned that a positive submission vote was not universal, they became very patriotic and generally receptive to militia service.(104)

Regionalism again played a role in the raising of troops for these campaigns. Easterners saw the raising of troops for the defense of the western frontiers as a drain on their economy, and not their prime concern. They were particularly incensed upon learning of the riots and march on Pittsburgh while General Wayne was preparing to attack the Indians in Ohio. However, when the call for Pennsylvania troops was made to put down the excise unrest in the West, more than one thousand of the five thousand troops (Pennsylvania's allotment) were from Philadelphia County. At first many eastern companies refused to march against their western brethren, but after federal officials disparaged the riots as detrimental to the union and detracting from national honor, the ranks began to swell. In the end, over twelve thousand troops were raised in just six weeks.(105)

On September 11 the vote was held in the western counties as to whether to submit to the laws or not. "A Friend of Peace" penned a letter to the Pittsburgh paper: "The awful question of Peace or a Civil War is to be decided by the people on the 11th instant, by an open public vote." The result was indecisive, due not only to the short notice given before the election but also to a misunderstanding as to who was to vote—only excise protesters, or the general population as well. In addition, many voters throughout the region took exception to the wording of the submission paper, which not only had the tone of a religious oath but also implied that all western inhabitants were rebels and had broken laws. Peace Commissioner James Ross put a notice in *The Pittsburgh Gazette* just five days before the vote: "Objections have been made to the words, 'Solemnly and Henceforth,' in the paper printed, and which is to be signed by the people on Thursday next. The Commissioners all agree that they may be struck out." There was no consistent method of reporting the results. While lists were made of signers in most townships of Washington, Allegheny, and Westmoreland counties, the Fayette County judges of election reported that a majority of those who voted were in favor of submission. However, voters represented only about a third of the voting population. The Fayette County Township Committees had met the day previous to the election and made the declarations required by the Standing Committee of Redstone. Therefore, they believed the voters were required only to answer yea or nay to the question of submission. (Ironmaster and Judge Isaac Meason requested Major Caleb Mountz to go and speak in favor of the Commissioner's terms at the meeting of the Fayette County townships of Bullskin and Tyrone. Mountz refused and stated, "There would be no army up—they would have sent an army to conquer the Indians if they could—it was only talked now to scare people.") There was no report from that part of Bedford County in the Fourth Survey. Consequently, it was unclear whether the citizens there knew to vote or not.(106)

Not receiving the necessary forms, many of the township groups creatively penned their own versions of the submission papers. Those from Smith Township, Washington County, added, "Reserving nevertheless full liberty in a constitutional and legal way to use every means and measure for obtaining a repeal of the excise law." The judges of West Bethlehem Township, Washington County, reported, "At least two thirds of the inhabitants met on the 11th—no answer could be obtained, neither affirmative or negative." Their neighbors from East Bethlehem Township answered with, "Peace with no Excise." All of the voters of Elizabeth Township, Allegheny County, in the forks of the Youghiogheny and Monongahela rivers, voted no. Those from Wheatfield Township, Westmoreland County, concluded,

"Although we dislike the excise law, yet we detest any riotous measure to oppose any law of our country and do recommend constitutional measures for its repeal to be first tried and fighting to be the last alternative." At other locations, such as Mingo Creek and Unity Township, Westmoreland County, voters were terrorized by those hostile to submission. The Commissioners reported that of the estimated eleven thousand taxable inhabitants in the Fourth Survey, twenty-seven hundred votes were tallied for submission. They noted, "Of these a very considerable part have not been subscribed in the mode agreed on—being either signed at a different day—unattested by any person or willfully varied from the settled form." They concluded that military strength would be necessary to execute the laws.(107)

On September 19 the Pennsylvania Assembly approved an act to suppress the insurrection in the western counties by calling out the militia. This action was belated as the first troops had already left Philadelphia. On the twenty-fourth the United States Commissioners made their recommendations for military action to the President. The following day Washington made a second proclamation in which he stated that it was time to remove those who would not submit to the laws of the United States. Militia forces from New Jersey, Pennsylvania, Maryland, and Virginia would be used to accomplish this. Between twelve and fifteen thousand men were raised in these four states to put down the Rebellion.(108)

"Accounts of the Western Expedition" show the federal troops were probably no better, and in some instances worse, in their discipline than the rebel militias at Braddock's Field. The bounty list of Captain Christian Hubbert's company of forty-seven men shows that three men had deserted before they crossed the Alleghenies, and another six men had been discharged before reaching the Pittsburgh area. It appears that at least two of Captain Conrad Seyfert's company were recruited from the Philadelphia prison. In October 1794 Lieutenant Colonel Joseph Cowperthwait reported to Governor Mifflin that while in camp at Bedford a private in Colonel Wentz's regiment "fired a musket which was loaded with small shott and wounded Sergeant Strup and David Wadington, two men in my regiment."(109)

In the meantime incidents of protest and sporadic violence occurred in diverse parts of the state. These occurred not only in the four western counties but also in these county seats: Bedford, Carlisle, Chambersburg, and Northumberland. These areas had at least two things in common: they produced a large amount of whiskey, and large segments of their inhabitants were of Scotch-Irish ancestry.(110)

By the end of September the federal army had arrived in Carlisle. This was not without incident. Between Myerstown, Lebanon County, and Carlisle two civilians were killed. When a detachment of the New Jersey cavalry entered Myerstown, a man, described as an itinerant, insulted an officer of the rear guard. A scuffle broke out when he refused to be placed under guard, and he was bayoneted by an old soldier. Another man, a member of a prominent Cumberland County family, was shot on the steps of a distillery near the village of Middlesex, just east of Carlisle, by a Pennsylvania dragoon. These incidents raised not only the fears of the western country but also those of Washington and Hamilton. Local displeasure was reflected in the increased price of goods to the army. Bedford local historian Vaughn Whisker said, "The army took over the town of Carlisle. One man was hard of hearing, walked out, and was killed. The people were mad as hell. They had to get the army out of there quick." Although Hamilton apologized for the killings to Governor Mifflin, he believed that the soldiers' actions were justified. The militia commanders were warned, however, to maintain the discipline of their troops. Hamilton lectured, "They cannot render a more important service to the cause of Government & order, than by a conduct scrupulously regardful of the rights of their fellow citizens."(111)

On October 2, township delegates from the western counties met for the second time at Parkinson's Ferry. They resolved not to oppose the excise laws. In addition, they appointed Congressman William Findley and lawyer and Washington County official David Redick to meet with President Washington to persuade him that it was not necessary to send troops to support the civil authority in the western country. Findley and Redick met with Washington on October 9. They were unable to convince him to stop the march of the army into the western country.

Antifederalist Congressman Findley of Westmoreland County wrote his personal account of the Rebellion in *History of the Insurrection in the Four Western Counties of Pennsylvania*, published in 1796. Not only was he concerned that an accurate record of the Rebellion be preserved, he also wanted to rectify what had already been written by his political opponents, particularly Hugh Brackenridge and Treasury Secretary Hamilton. Findley saw himself as one to restore order not only at the excise meetings but also in his home area of Westmoreland County. In an earlier letter to Secretary Hamilton, Clymer had described Findley as the "father of all the disturbances of the Western Country." It was for this judgment that Brackenridge reasoned that the Committee's choice of Findley had been unwise.(112)

President Washington arrived at Carlisle on October 4. He had not wanted to formalize his plans until he reached there. Washington wrote on September 28, "I shall leave the City the day after tomorrow for Carlisle, to decide there, at a nearer view, whether to proceed with the troops against the Insurgents." He reviewed the troops from New Jersey and Pennsylvania there, and the mood of the town changed with his appearance. The President, who breathed a sense of his power and the majesty of his office to the troops and civilians, was given a royal welcome by the troops and the local citizens alike. Detailed newspaper accounts of the President's reception there were communicated to the East and throughout the nation. The road would become the civic stage as the troops headed west, perhaps the first and last such civic procession across the state. Secretary of the Commonwealth Alexander J. Dallas (1759-1817) wrote, "On Friday, Saturday and Sunday, about 7500 men took up the line of march...and when I saw the President lift his hat to the troops as they passed along, I thought I caught a glimpse of

Front elevation of "The Meadows," the c. 1810 house of U.S. Senator and peace commissioner James Ross, which stood in O'Hara Township, Allegheny County, until it was demolished in the 1930s.

the Revolutionary Scene." Although Dallas was a member of the Democratic Society of Pennsylvania, his journal writings indicate he was ever ready to malign the rebels.(113)

George Washington, national hero of the Revolution and first president of the nation, retained the respect and esteem of a majority of its citizens. This was used with great effect during the march west. Having had dealings with the people of western Pennsylvania since the time of the French and Indian War, and being an extensive landholder there, Washington had preconceived notions of their motives and loyalty to the nation. His experiences had found the people to be crude, ignorant, and land grabbing. James Ross, who Washington appointed as one of his peace commissioners, was also his western Pennsylvania land agent. Washington would be among those to benefit from the rise in land values after the Rebellion. Washington exemplified the Federalist belief that a display of force was necessary, not only to show the westerners but the world that his government was committed to a lasting union.(114)

The New Jersey and Pennsylvania troops, along with the Washington entourage, marched from Carlisle on October 11. In Chambersburg, "the people were at their doors and the president acknowledged their salutations as he rode along the streets on horseback, followed by his black servant carrying a large portmanteau." Beyond Chambersburg, the President headed south toward Fort Cumberland while the right column of the army took the Forbes Road west. Washington arrived at Fort Cumberland, Maryland, on the sixteenth where he reviewed the troops from Virginia and Maryland. The two branches of the army arrived in Bedford on the nineteenth. Before returning to Philadelphia, Washington left the army in the hands of the noted cavalryman and his friend from the Revolution, General Henry Lee (1756-1818). Washington instructed Lee as to the purposes and procedures of the army in the western counties. This mission included the suppression of opposition to the excise laws and the execution of the laws. These objectives were to be effected in two ways, by military force and by judiciary process. The army was marched in two columns using the most convenient routes, with Parkinson's Ferry as its destination. Lee's successful and relatively peaceful quelling of the uprising helped restore faith in the national government, but evidently shortened his career as governor of Virginia.(115)

Instead of resistance, the troops were met only with the sullen defiance of "liberty poles" erected along the army's route. Realizing how hard it was to raise troops to fight the Indians, westerners could not comprehend a force being raised to subdue them. It would leave a bitter taste in the memories of western Pennsylvanians for generations. However, it had been just as remarkable that over seven thousand rebel militiamen assembled on a weekend and marched on Pittsburgh. At the end of October, Secretary Dallas wrote from Bonnet's Camp, "But fifteen thousand men have been marched three hundred miles, without a symptom of opposition; and they are, at this moment, in the heart of the enemy's country, with plenty around them of everything, but avowed enemies." Dallas also felt there was no remorse on the part of the opposition. He declared, "The pole has been taken down; but it is obvious that the disposition which set it up, has not been subdued." (116)

Meanwhile the regular fall elections took place on October 14. In the congressional district adjacent to his own, comprising Allegheny and Washington counties, Albert Gallatin was elected to the House of Representatives. Historian Henry Adams attributed this to the people's belief that the preservation of peace was due to Gallatin's courage and character during the excise meetings. Federalist opponents claimed that the election was invalid because the western counties were in a state of insurrection. They mustered enough support in Congress to declare the election invalid, but the new election resulted in Gallatin's re-election. In spite of, or perhaps because he was labeled a foreigner by his political opponents, he was much beloved by his western constituents and would continue to be a spokesman for these rural farmers into the late 1790s.(117)

The final meeting of the committees of townships was held at Parkinson's Ferry on October 24. The resolves drawn up there were sent to the President through four representatives. They announced that the civil authorities were now competent to enforce the laws, and that any offender should surrender himself to the authorities.

By November 1 both columns of the army had crossed the Allegheny Mountains. The left column under General Lee arrived at Uniontown, and members of the right column reached Pittsburgh. On November 8, General Lee, camped near Parkinson's Ferry, issued a proclamation to the inhabitants of the four western counties. He declared that the armies which they saw surrounding them were there because of the determination of the people of the United States to uphold the government they had established. He recommended that the people accommodate the army, take an oath to support the constitution, and obey the laws. A day later, Lee provided General Irvine with a list of descriptions to identify insurgents. In addition, he disclosed a list of offenders and witnesses to be apprehended. What would be termed the "dreadful night" occurred four days later. Based on the fear of another exodus from the country, arrests were made of approximately 150 suspects and witnesses in the middle of that night. In some cases, men were brutally dragged out of bed, half-clothed, and marched through mud to cold, makeshift prison quarters. At least one man died from exposure to the cold. Charles Smith wrote from Pittsburgh on the thirteenth, "Detachments of horse were scattered in every Direction and at the same instant acted against the objects who were marked out."(118)

"The Terrible Night" illustrating the rainy/snowy night during which suspected whiskey rebels were rounded up by federal troops.

By the middle of November, the excise tax collectors who had returned with the army began seizing the stills of those who had not registered them. On November 20, Supervisor Neville opened a collection office in each of the four counties.

Encountering no real opposition and with the arrests of suspected insurrectionists accomplished, the main body of the army began its march back east on November 19. Samuel Stotler, whose father had a tavern near Reel's Corner in Shade Township, Somerset County, recalled the return of the army on the Pennsylvania Road. He said the mud was almost knee deep and half the troops were "beastly drunk." "The troopers took possession of everything they could get their hands upon." Ironmaster George Anshutz failed in his attempt to manufacture iron near Pittsburgh in 1794 because the federal soldiers stole his supply of cordwood intended for use as charcoal.(119)

Because the Parkinson's Ferry area was a center of unrest, a force of men under General Daniel Morgan went into winter camp at the mouth of Lobb's Run. Small detachments were also placed at Pittsburgh and Washington. The camp at Lobb's Run was swept with smallpox, which resulted in the death of several men, two of whom are buried in Lobb's Cemetery. Six days later about eighteen of the suspected insurgents and their guards started their trek to Philadelphia. The troops, with their prisoners, arrived in Philadelphia on Christmas Day, 1794. They were greeted with artillery discharges, the ringing of bells, and a huge crowd on Broad Street.(120)

On November 19, President Washington addressed Congress concerning the Whiskey Insurrection. He explained his actions to "protect and defend the Constitution of the United States." Ten days later, General Lee issued his proclamation of pardon to all persons in the counties of Washington, Allegheny, Westmoreland, and Fayette in the state of Pennsylvania, and Ohio County, Virginia, except twenty-eight men in Pennsylvania and five in Virginia.(121)

Epilogue

Trials of those accused of crimes during the Rebellion began in Philadelphia in May. Accounts vary, but at least forty-three men were tried on charges ranging from misdemeanor to treason. (Although the descriptions vary and often coincide with the charges of treason, those charged with the lesser crime of misdemeanor appear to be those "seditious" persons who "assembled and confederated to raise an insurrection.") Twelve of those who were found guilty had fled the region. Much of the evidence against the suspected rebels could not be substantiated in court. In many cases, witnesses could not be found to support the allegations of the national government. The tone of the government charges betrays the near fanatical light in which the government saw the rebels and their actions. For example, the charges against Carlisle tailor William Peterkin continually rail against "wicked, evil disposed, and seditious persons." Peterkin was accused of attending a liberty pole raising in Carlisle in mid-September. At that time he "maliciously, advisedly wickedly, and seditiously, openly and publicly uttered and published the false, wicked and seditious words following, 'That the Glorious Sons of Liberty to the West ought not to be faulted for what they had done but applauded and supported.'"(122)

No influential men were among those tried for treason. In the end, of the twenty-four prisoners, only John Mitchell and Philip Wigle were sentenced to die. Mitchell, who had robbed the mail, and Wigle, who had participated in a riot in Fayette County, were both described as "simple" men. A witness to their trial, Dr. Christian Boerster of Berlin, Somerset County, pictured these poor men with small children as really having no knowledge of how the uprising started. He charged that the real traitors were the spectators and judges at these trials. Washington later pardoned all except David Bradford.(123)

The Whiskey Rebellion set several precedents which were established by interpretation of the United States Constitution and the laws authenticated by it. Among the points of law in need of definition was the act of treason against the United States. The Rebellion resulted in the first arrests and trials for treason in the federal courts. These trials established the precedent that armed opposition to the execution of a United States statute was equal to "levying war" against the United States and thus was within the constitutional definition of treason. United States District Attorney William Rawle's interpretation of English common law that "raising a body of men to obtain, by intimidation or violence, the repeal of a law, is an act of levying war" was confirmed in Justice William Paterson's summation to the jury and became a part of American law. (Rawle, appointed by Washington, acted as prosecutor of the alleged whiskey rebels, and Paterson, a justice of the United States Supreme Court, sat for the trials of alleged whiskey rebels at the Federal District Court for the District of Pennsylvania held in York, Pennsylvania, in 1795.)(124)

The judges in these trials unmistakably aided the national government in its cases. Judge Richard Peters thought that the federal judiciary should not be hampered by state procedures. In particular, he opined, "It never could have been in the contemplation of congress, by any reference to state regulations, to defeat the operation of the national laws." In other words, these trials established the primacy of federal law over state law. In addition, Justice Paterson seems to usurp the jury's fact-finding function by stating that there was no doubt as to the direction the evidence pointed, leaving no discretion for the jury.(125)

The Whiskey Rebellion was also the first time a chief executive of the United States nationalized military forces to suppress an internal political upheaval. This set a precedent that would be used again in 1799 by President John Adams during the Fries Rebellion in eastern Pennsylvania, and later by President Abraham Lincoln with the outbreak of the Civil War in 1861.(126)

The Whiskey Rebellion not only set precedents in establishing the legal jurisdiction of the national government, but also instituted the settlement and containment of the frontier within the union of states as a priority. In addition, the Rebellion served to coalesce the two political factions emerging from the Revolution into a two-party system. It also helped define the nation's economic interests as it struggled to evolve from a fundamentally agricultural society to a growing commercial/industrial system.

Many of the participants in the Rebellion had gained political and military experience during the Revolution. The Rebellion was also the training ground and turning point in the careers of many politicians, some for the better, some for the worse. The Rebellion marked the height of the strength of the Federalist party, and the career of its greatest spokesman, Alexander Hamilton. State leaders such as Albert Gallatin and Hugh Brackenridge, through their oratorical skills, were able to moderate the course of the Rebellion and subsequently advanced in their careers. While most local leaders of the rebels stayed and became or continued as local officials or judges, many of the common laborers and farmers who participated in the Rebellion moved further on into the frontier in their search for the American dream of land and freedom. "But we receive daily accounts of numbers that are endeavoring to save themselves by flight," wrote Secretary Dallas in late October. "Boats, loaded with fugitives are constantly passing down the Ohio."(127)

The Rebellion illustrated the traditional concern for the property rights of the economic and political elite as opposed to the human rights of the common citizen. Although there is repeated mention of compensation for the losses of personal property by excise collectors and their supporters, there is no reference made to recompense for the loss of life during the Rebellion. At least three protesters were killed at Neville's house, and two civilians were killed by the federal troops. In addition, a soldier from Fort Fayette was killed at Neville's, and an unknown number of men died on the march west or at encampments. (The journals of soldiers and civilians, along with governmental reports, indicate a high number of sickly soldiers in camp and at the military hospitals established at Bedford and Pittsburgh.) At least one suspected rebel died as a result of inhumane treatment during his confinement, and Herman Husband died before he could reach home. On the other hand, the rebel leaders showed remarkable restraint in preventing the deaths of any excise collectors or their advocates. Despite the opportunity for total mayhem at Neville's and the march on Pittsburgh, even those accused of being the most radical went to considerable length in exercising what they considered honorable behavior. For example, David Hamilton allowed Major Kirkpatrick to escape from Neville's, and Colonel David Philips permitted Marshal Lennox to depart undetected later that evening.(128)

For the time being regionalism had lost. The Federalist revolutionaries of 1776, now acting as conservatives, had taken the same position their British predecessors had, while the western rebels voiced the identical ideology and claims of self-interest that had been advanced by all segments of America in 1776. The increase of currency in the region through military spending, the release of dissatisfied settlers further onto the frontier, the pacification of the Ohio Indians with the 1795 Treaty of Greenville, the opening of the Mississippi River through the 1795 Pinckney Treaty, and the release of British forts of the Northwest through the Jay Treaty undoubtedly quelled western unrest more than the army. Financially, the excise tax had been a dismal failure. The military expedition alone ran up a bill of $1,500,000, or about one-third of all the money that was received for the ten-year period the act was in effect. Indeed, the events of 1794 shaped the course of future events for the region and the country.(129)

The Federalists would continue in power for six more years, and there is some evidence that the Whiskey Rebellion experience taught them how to better govern. Excise collectors were instructed to be forgiving and patient of distillers. Tench Coxe, Commissioner of Revenue for the Treasury Department, advised Thomas Marshall, Supervisor of Ohio, "to produce all such measures in Kentucky, as will wind up, with *promptness* and *Harmony*, the business prior to July 1794." The Rebellion was the turning point in the career of Jefferson, Madison, and Gallatin, all of whom would come to power in 1801 with Jefferson's election. The excise tax was repealed the following year. While Federalist policies tended to enslave agriculturalists to commercial powers, Jefferson would seek to elevate the farmer, the "chosen people of God." Jefferson argued that "the establishment and survival of democracy depended on peopling the land predominantly with farmers."(130)

The Whiskey Rebellion is significant for several reasons. By the 1790s, post-Revolutionary events in American government were leading to a confrontation as two ideological groups coalesced. Prior to the development of the two-party system, there were few channels for expression of dissatisfaction with the sitting government. Western people and their leaders used the methods they had known previously—extralegal meetings which resulted in petitions for redress and community censure. The officials of the young democracy had to gain experience in governing, and people living on the frontier needed to learn that they could not live in total freedom and still enjoy the privileges of national citizenship.

TO WHISKEY

BY A SCOTS-IRISHMAN.

Great Pow'r that warms the heart and liver,
And puts the bluid a' in a fever,
If dull and heartlefs I am ever,
  A blaft o' thee
Makes me as blyth, and brifk, and clever
  As only bee.

I wat ye are a cunning chiel,
O' a' your tricks I ken fu' weel,
For aft ye hae gien me a heel,
  And thrown me down,
When I fhook hands wi' heart fo leel'
  Ye wily loun.

Poem, "To Whiskey," written in the Scotch-Irish dialect by David Bruce, who was a resident of Washington County in 1794.

Notes

(1) Hugh H. Brackenridge, *Incidents of the Insurrection in the Western Parts of Pennsylvania in the year 1794* (Philadelphia: John M'Culloch, 1795), p. 5.

(2) James P. McClure, "The Ends of the American Earth: Pittsburgh and the Upper Ohio Valley to 1795," Vol. I (PhD. dissertation, University of Michigan, 1983), p. 658; T. J. C. Williams and Folger McKinsey, *History of Frederick County, Maryland*, Vol. I (Baltimore: Regional Publishing Co., 1979), pp. 140-141; J. Thomas Scharf, *History of Maryland*, Vol. II (Baltimore: John B. Piet, 1879), p. 585.

(3) John B. Linn and William H. Egle, eds., *Pennsylvania Archives, Second Series*, Vol. IV (Harrisburg: B. F. Meyers, State Printer, 1876), pp. 391-392; *The Oracle of Dauphin and Harrisburgh Advertiser*, October 6, 1794; George R. Beyer, *Guide to the State Historical Markers of Pennsylvania* (Harrisburg: Pennsylvania Historical and Museum Commission, 1991), pp. 39, 59-60, 103.

(4) David Thelan, "Memory and American History," *The Journal of American History*, Vol. 75, No. 4, March 1989, pp. 1122-1127.

(5) Interview with Vaughn Whisker, August 7, 1990.

(6) Interview with William Defibaugh, August 8, 1990.

(7) Canon Richard Davies, talk on Whiskey Rebellion tour, March 28, 1993.

(8) Interview with Gilbert Balliard, November 15, 1990.

(9) Henry Christopher McCook, *The Latimers: A Tale of the Western Insurrection of 1794* (Philadelphia: G. W. Jacobs & Co., 1898), p. 4.

(10) Conversation with Irk McConnell, March 18, 1992 and April 20, 1993; Elizabeth J. Wall, *Men of the Whiskey Insurrection in Southwestern Pennsylvania* (Pittsburgh, 1988), p. 34; Dorothy E. Fennell, "From Rebelliousness to Insurrection: A Social History of the Whiskey Rebellion, 1765-1802" (PhD. dissertation, University of Pittsburgh, 1981), pp. 157-158; Boyd Crumrine, ed., *History of Washington County, Pennsylvania* (Philadelphia: L. H. Everts & Co., 1882), p. 702.

(11) Interview with Miller Barb, April 23, 1992.

(12) Thomas P. Slaughter, *The Whiskey Rebellion: Frontier Epilogue to the American Revolution* (New York: Oxford University Press, 1986), pp. 221, 227; Fennell, pp. 1-4; See Edward Countryman, *A People in Revolution: The American Revolution and Political Society in New York 1760-1790* (Baltimore: Johns Hopkins University Press, 1981).

(13) Morris J. Vogel, *Cultural Connections: Museums and Libraries of Philadelphia and the Delaware Valley* (Philadelphia: Temple University Press, 1991), pp. 33-38.

(14) *History of Bedford, Somerset, and Fulton Counties, Pennsylvania with Illustrations and biographical Sketches* (Chicago: A. Warner & Co., 1884), p. 459; Mark H. Jones, "Herman Husband: Millenarian, Carolina Regulator, and Whiskey Rebel" (PhD. Dissertation for Northern Illinois University, 1982). R. D. W. Connor, *History of North Carolina*, Vol. 1 (Chicago and New York: Lewis Publishing Co., 1919), p. 302.

(15) David P. Szatmary, *Shays' Rebellion: The Making of an Agrarian Insurrection* (Amherst: University of Massachusetts Press, 1980), pp. 37, 39, 56.

(16) Ibid., p. 119.

(17) Joseph J. Ellis, *After the Revolution: Profiles of Early American Culture* (New York: W. W. Norton & Co., 1979), p. 80.

(18) Fennell, pp. 179-180; Williams and McKinsey, p. 140; 1798 Federal Tax, List B, Salem Township, Westmoreland County; Stevenson W. Fletcher, *Pennsylvania Agriculture and Country Life, 1640-1840* (Harrisburg: Pennsylvania Historical and Museum Commission, 1950), p. 290.

(19) Slaughter, pp. 57-59, 88-89.

(20) Ibid., pp. 39-40; Ellis, pp. 102, 107, 109.

(21) Fletcher, pp. 147, 151; David John Jeremy, ed., *Henry Wansey and His American Journal, 1794* (Philadelphia: American Philosophical Society, 1970), p. 38; Amos Long, Jr., *The Pennsylvania German Family Farm* (Breinigsville: The Pennsylvania German Society, 1972), p. 171; *The Oxford English Dictionary*, Second Edition, Vol. XIV (Oxford: Clarendon Press, 1989), p. 308.

(22) Szatmary, p. 58; *Old Overholt: The History of a Whiskey*, Carnegie Library of Pittsburgh, p. 6; David C. Knight, *The Whiskey Rebellion, 1794: Revolt in Pennsylvania Threatens American Unity* (New York: Franklin Watts, Inc., 1968), p. 19; Slaughter, pp. 215, 224.

(23) Tench Coxe, *A Statement of the Arts and Manufacturing of the United States of America, for the year 1810* (Philadelphia: A. Cornman, 1814), p. xiii; David J. Cuff, William J. Young, Edward K. Muller, Wilbur Zelinsky, and Ronald F. Abler, eds., *The Atlas of Pennsylvania* (Philadelphia: Temple University Press, 1989), p. 94; *The Seventh Census of the United States*, 1850 Agricultural Returns, Census of 1840 (Washington: Robert Armstrong, Public Printer, 1853), p. lxxxv.

(24) Adam Seybert, *Statistical Annals*, etc. (New York: Burt Franklin, 1969), p. 463.

(25) Boyd Crumrine, ed., *History of Washington County, Pennsylvania* (Philadelphia: L. H. Everts & Co., 1882), p. 265; Fletcher, p. 290; R. Eugene Harper, "Fayette County, 1783-1790: A Study of the Economic Base and Local Government" (Master's Thesis for University of Pittsburgh, 1962), pp. 53-54; Fennell, pp. 148, 160.

(26) John Neville Papers, Letter Book, Microfilm P-273, Carnegie Library of Pittsburgh.

(27) Pittsburgh *Gazette*, November 13, 1812 and April 2, 1813; *A. Overholt & Co.: A History of the Company and the Overholt Family*, August, 1940, Carnegie Library of Pittsburgh, pp. 15-22; *Highlights of Large Whiskey*, Carnegie Library of Pittsburgh, pp. 2-7; Marion Tinling and Godfrey Davies, eds., *The Western Country in 1793: Reports on Kentucky and Virginia by Harry Toulmin* (San Marino, Calif.: Castle Press, 1948), p. 102; Long, p. 168; Edwin Morris Betts, *Thomas Jefferson's Farm Book: With Commentary and Relevant Extracts from Other Writings* (Charlottesville: University Press of Virginia, 1976), 415; John S. Van Voorhis, *The Old and New Monongahela* (Pittsburgh: Nicholson Printer, 1893), p.14.

(28) Rev. William Hanna, *History of Greene County, Pennsylvania* (Greensboro, Pa., 1882), pp. 25, 111; Agreement dated April 6, 1793 between William Bartlett of Westmoreland County and Abraham Whipple of Marietta County, Northwest Territory, Thomas Hamilton Collection, Westmoreland County Historical Society, Greensburg.

(29) Sylvester K. Stevens, *Pennsylvania: Titan of Industry,* Vol. I (New York: Lewis Historical Publishing Co., Inc., 1948), p. 111; *Kline's Carlisle Weekly Gazette,* Carlisle, January 29, 1794; *Gazette of the United States and Daily Evening Advertiser,* Philadelphia, John Fenno, publisher, July, August, 1794; *General Advertiser,* Philadelphia, Benjamin Franklin Bache, publisher, July, August, 1794; Brackenridge, p. 21.

(30) Tinling and Davies, pp. 107, 113; D. Clayton James, *Antebellum Natchez* (Baton Rouge: Louisiana State University Press, 1968), p. 44.

(31) Madeline Sapienza, *Modern Chivalry in Early American Law: H. H. Brackenridge's Legal Thought* (Lanham/New York/London: University Press of America, 1992), p. 20.

(32) McClure, p. 151; Fennell, p. 42.

(33) Jackson Turner Main, *The Antifederalists: Critics of the Constitution 1781-1788* (New York: W. W. Norton & Co., 1961), pp. 41-47; Vogel, p. 28; William A. Hunter, "The French and Indian War and the Revolution," *Pennsylvania Heritage,* Vol II, No. 3, June 1976, p. 9.

(34) H. M. Brackenridge, *Recollections of Persons and Places in the West* (Philadelphia: J. B. Lippincott & Co., 1868), p. 109; Henry Adams, *The Life of Albert Gallatin* (New York: Peter Smith, 1943), pp. 146-147.

(35) Leland D. Baldwin, *Whiskey Rebels: The Story of a Frontier Uprising* (Pittsburgh: University of Pittsburgh Press, 1939), p. 93; Rayner W. Kelsey, ed., *Cazenove Journal 1794: A Record of the Journey of Theophile Cazenove Through New Jersey and Pennsylvania* (Haverford: Pennsylvania History Press, 1922) p.10.

(36) James, pp. 48-59.

(37) Harper, p. 75; George E. Connor, "The Politics of Insurrection: A Comparative Analysis of the Shays', Whiskey, and Fries' Rebellions," *The Social Science Journal,* Vol. 29, No.3, 1992, p. 268; Yves-Marie Berce, translated by Joseph Bergin, *Revolt and Revolution in Early Modern Europe: An Essay on the History of Political Violence* (Manchester: Manchester University Press, 1987).

(38) Fennell, pp. 76-93; Buck and Buck, pp. 264-265, 279, 284-287.

(39) *Kline's Carlisle Weekly Gazette,* Carlisle, July 9, 1794.

(40) James, p. 43.

(41) *Gazette of the United States and Daily Evening Advertiser,* Philadelphia, August 2, 1794; *General Advertiser*, Philadelphia, August 4, 1794; Letter from a Yellow Breeches Farmer, *Kline's Carlisle Weekly Gazette,* Carlisle, September 17, 1794; Wayland F. Dunaway, *Scotch-Irish of Colonial Pennsylvania* (Hamden, Ct.: Archon Books, 1962), pp. 73-77; Administrative Account of James McFarlane Estate, Law Library of Washington County Courthouse; Maldwyn A. Jones, "Ulster Emigration, 1783-1815," *Essays in Scotch-Irish History*, E.R.R. Green, ed. (London: Routledge & Kegan Paul, 1969), p. 63. In the conflict between Federalists and Republicans, the Scotch-Irish were overwhelmingly on the side of the Jeffersonians, whose sympathies were with Republican France. Not only did Scotch-Irish immigrants share these sympathies, but they instinctively hated the Federalists as would-be aristocrats and as tools of the British.

(42) Baldwin, pp. 16-17, 49, 205; Joseph Smith, D.D., *Old Redstone; or, Historical Sketches of Western Presbyterianism, Its Early Ministers, Its Perilous Times, and Its First Records* (Philadelphia: Lippincott, Grambo & Co., 1854), p. 251; Rev. John McMillan tombstone in Chartiers Hill Presbyterian Churchyard; Esmond Wright, "Education in the American Colonies: The Impact of Scotland," *Essays in Scotch-Irish History, p. 23.*

(43) Fennell, pp. 92-93; Robert Porter Trial Transcript, May 18, 1795, MSS Collection of Historical Society of Western Pennsylvania.

(44) Microfilm M986 Reel 1, *Criminal Case Files of the U.S. Circuit Court for the Eastern District of Pennsylvania, 1791-1840,* Roll 1, Case Files, 1791-1799.

(45) Wallace Guy Smeltzer, *Methodism on the Headwaters of the Ohio,* (Nashville: Parthenon Press, 1951), pp. 75-80.

(46) Fennell, pp. 193-226; R. D. W. Connor, p. 304; Jones, p. 349.

(47) Malcolm J. Rohrbough, *The Trans-Appalachian Frontier: People, Societies, and Institutions, 1775-1850* (New York: Oxford University Press, 1978), p. 7; Fennell, pp. 46-74.

(48) Fennell, pp. 151-152.

(49) Hugh Henry Brackenridge, *Incidents of the Insurrection,*Daniel Marder, ed., (New Haven, Conn.: College and University Press, 1972), p. 143; Edward Countryman, *A People in Revolution: The American Revolution and Political Society in New York 1760-1790* (Baltimore: Johns Hopkins University Press, 1981), p. 294; Connor, pp. 270-272.

(50) *The Pittsburgh Gazette*, August 23, 1794; Pennsylvania State Archives, Harrisburg, RG-4, *Records of the Office of the Controller General, Western Expedition (Whiskey Rebellion) Accounts 1794-1804,* List of Men's Names in Capt. Christian Hubbert's Company who received Bounty, January 17, 1795.

(51) Fennell, pp. 9-10, 101, 165; I. Daniel Rupp, *History and Topography of Dauphin, Cumberland, Franklin, Bedford, Adams and Perry Counties,* (Lancaster: Gilbert Hills, Proprietor & Publisher, 1846), pp. 475-481; *The Oxford English Dictionary,* Vol. V, Second Edition (Oxford: Clarendon Press, 1989), p. 609; Conversation with Dorothy Fennell, January 22, 1993; Bernard A. Weisberger, "Seeking A Real Tax Revolt," *American Heritage,* May/June 1991, p. 22.

(52) Richard Peters, Esq., ed., *Public Statutes At Large of the United States of America,* Vol. I (Boston: Charles C. Little and James Brown, 1848), pp. 199-214; Slaughter, p. 99.

(53) Baldwin, p. 82; Francis Wharton, *State Trials of the United States During the Administrations of Washington and Adams with References, Historical and Professional, and Preliminary Notes on the Politics of the Times,* (Philadelphia: Carey and Hart, 1849), p. 105, Robert Johnson charged John Robertson, John Hamilton, and Thomas McComb for the tarring and feathering he received on Pigeon Creek.

(54) Pennsylvania Whiskey Rebellion Collection, 1792-96 MS 16,804 Library of Congress, 1976.

(55) Linn and Egle, pp. 32-33; Slaughter, p. 122; Pennsylvania Whiskey Rebellion Collection, William Faulkner testified September 28, 1792 that the following men assembled at the house of Josiah Tannehill on August 21: Col. John Canon, Col. John Hamilton, Benjamin Parkinson, Col. James Marshall, Sheshbazzer Bentley, David Bradford, Albert Gallatin, John Smiley, Edward Cook, Esq., Mr. Philips, and Neal Gillespie.

(56) Adams, pp. 93-94.

(57) John Catanzariti, ed., *The Papers of Thomas Jefferson,* Vol. 24, "Notes of a Conversation with George Washington, July 10, 1792" and "Letter from George Washington, September 15, 1792" (Princeton: Princeton University Press, 1990), pp. 210-211, 383-384.

(58) Peters, pp. 271-274; Fennell, pp. 60-74.

(59) Harold C. Syrett, ed., *The Papers of Alexander Hamilton,* Vol. XII (New York: Columbia University Press, 1967), pp. 305-310, 495-497, 540-542; Smeltzer, p. 77.

(60) Edward Everett, "John Smilie, Forgotten Champion of Early Western Pennsylvania," *The Western Pennsylvania Historical Magazine,* Vol. 33, Sept.-Dec. 1950, p. 89; Linn and Egle, p. 287.

(61) Syrett, p. 312.

(62) Letter, William Findley to Thomas Hamilton, November 28, 1792, Thomas Hamilton Collection, Westmoreland County Historical Society.

(63) Fennell, pp. 129-133.

(64) Microfilm M986 Reel 1; Slaughter, p. 151.

(65) *History of Allegheny County, Pennsylvania* (Chicago: A. Warner & Co. Publishers, 1889), p. 156; Fennell, p. 98.

(66) McClure, pp. 578-593, 820-821.

(67) Baldwin, pp. 52, 95, 282; McClure, p. 580; William Findley, *History of the Insurrection in the Four Western Counties of Pennsylvania* (Spartanburg, S.C.: Reprint Co., 1984), pp. 56-57.

(68) Joseph F. McFarlane, *20th Century History of the City of Washington and Washington County and Representative Citizens* (Chicago: Richmond-Arnold Pub. Co., 1910), p. 107.

(69) James Tagg, *Benjamin Franklin Bache and the Philadelphia Aurora* (Philadelphia: University of Pennsylvania Press, 1991), pp. 207-210.

(70) Letter George Clymer to Robert Johnson, March 8, 1794, MSS Collection of U. Grant Miller Library, Washington and Jefferson College.

(71) Peters, pp. 384-390; See Roland Baumann, "Philadelphia's Manufacturers and the Excise Tax of 1794: The Forging of the Jeffersonian Coalition," *The Whiskey Rebellion: Past and Present Perspectives*, Steven R. Boyd, ed. (Westport, Conn.: Greenwood Press, 1985), pp. 135-164.

(72) Baldwin, pp. 101-102; Fennell, pp. 108-109; Historical Society of Washington County, MSS Collection.

(73) Linn and Egle, p. 160; Porter Trial Transcript.

(74) Slaughter, p. 179; Baldwin, p. 115; Brackenridge, p. 122; Oliver Miller Homestead printed leaflet, 1992.

(75) Slaughter, pp. 150-153; Fennell, pp. 124-126; The September 3, 1794 issue of *Kline's Carlisle Weekly Gazette* reports that a party of armed and blacked men called on Major Huling, Collector of Excise for Cumberland County. After obtaining his commission and papers, the party went off without further injury.

(76) Washington County Court Accounts, James McFarlane Estate Inventory.

(77) Brackenridge, p. 19; Syrett, Vol. XVII, p. 4; Pennsylvania Whiskey Rebellion Collection, undated letter Alexander Fulton to George Washington.

(78) Baldwin, pp. 102-103, 127; Slaughter, pp. 184-185; Adams, p. 149.

(79) McClure, p. 594; Linn and Egle, p. 111.

(80) Oliver Wolcott, p. 14.

(81) Adams, pp. 149-150; Linn and Egle, p. 63.

(82) John Neville Papers, Letter Book, Microfilm P-273, Carnegie Library of Pittsburgh.

(83) Baldwin, pp. 159, 162-164; *The Pittsburgh Gazette,* August 2, 1794.

(84) *The Pittsburgh Gazette,* August 16, 1794, and September 6, 1794.

(85) Brackenridge, p. 16; McClure, pp. 617-619; Sapienza, p. 21.

(86) Pennsylvania Whiskey Rebellion Collection, Letter August 5, 1794, Thomas Mifflin to George Washington; Linn and Egle, pp. 104-111, 148-154; Wayne L. Trotta, "James Wilson: Forgotten Founding Father," *Pennsylvania Heritage*, Vol XVIII, No. 4, Fall 1992, p. 20.

(87) Pennsylvania State Archives, County Militia Accounts.

(88) Linn and Egle, pp. 13, 123-127; Tagg, p. 214.

(89) McClure, p. 636; Baldwin, pp. 103, 179; Fennell, p. 117; Microfilm M986 Reel 1, United States vs. William Bonham, Thomas Caldwell, Alexander Fulton, Thomas Gaddis, William Peterkin, John Wray, etc.; *Kline's Weekly Carlisle Gazette,* Carlisle, August 20, 1794; J. Thomas Scharf, *History of Western Maryland: Being a History of Frederick, Montgomery, Carroll, Washington, Allegheny, and Garrett counties*, Vol. II (Philadelphia: Louis H. Everts, 1882), p. 1069.

(90) *General Advertiser*, Philadelphia, August 25, 1794; *Gazette of the United States and Daily Evening Advertiser,* Philadelphia, August 20, 1794; Tagg, p.215.

(91) D. Wilson Thompson, *Early Publications of Carlisle, Pennsylvania 1785-1835* (Carlisle: The Sentinel, 1932), pp. 2, 5; *Kline's Carlisle Weekly Gazette*, Carlisle, September 3, 1794.

(92) *The Pittsburgh Gazette*, August-September, 1794; McClure, pp. 633, 658.

(93) Adams, pp. 87-89, 130-135; Gallatin, p. 27.

(94) Adams, pp. 134-135; The Papers of Albert Gallatin, Microfilm Roll 44: 721-722, August 14, 1848, William Beach Lawrence to B. K. Stevens.

(95) Linn and Egle, pp. 32-33.

(96) Albert Gallatin, *The Speech of Albert Gallatin, a Representative from the County of Fayette, in the House of Representatives of the General Assembly of Pennsylvania, on the Important Question Touching the Validity of the Elections Held in the Four Western counties of the State, on the 14th day of October, 1794. With Notes and an Appendix Containing Sundry Documents Relative to the Western Insurrection* (Philadelphia: William W. Woodword,

1795); The Papers of Albert Gallatin, Microfilm Roll 44: 154, August 20, 1846, Albert Gallatin to Ezekiel Bacon.

(97) McClure, p. 619; Connor, p. 260.

(98) Pennsylvania Whiskey Rebellion Collection, Letter August 17, 1794, United States Commissioners to the Secretary of State.

(99) Pennsylvania Whiskey Rebellion Collection, Letter September 5, 1794, Jasper Yeates and William Bradford to the Secretary of State.

(100) Baldwin, p. 220.

(101) Slaughter, pp. 209-210. Thomas J. C. Williams, *A History of Washington County, Maryland: From the Earliest Settlements to the Present Time* (Baltimore: Regional Publishing Co., 1968), p. 113; Scharf, *History of Maryland*, p. 583.

(102) Linn and Egle, p. 237; Richard A. Ifft, "Treason in the Early Republic: The Federal Courts, Popular Protest, and Federalism During the Whiskey Insurrection," *The Whiskey Rebellion: Past and Present Perspectives,* Steven R. Boyd, ed. (Westport, Conn.: Greenwood Press, 1985), p. 167.

(103) Linn and Egle, pp. 259-261; Adams, p. 138.

(104) Linn and Egle, pp. 280-282.

(105) *Gazette of the United States and Daily Evening Advertiser,* Philadelphia, August 12, 1794.

(106) Pennsylvania Whiskey Rebellion Collection, Report of the Committee of Townships, Fayette County, September 10, 1794, Albert Gallatin, secretary, and election returns from the various townships; *The Pittsburgh Gazette*, September 6, 1794; Microfilm M986 Reel 1, Deposition of Isaac Meason before Richard Peters, Esq. November 29, 1794.

(107) Pennsylvania Whiskey Rebellion Collection, Report of the United States Commissioners, and election returns from the various townships; Baldwin, pp. 209-215.

(108) Linn and Egle, pp. 348-359.

(109) Irvine Papers, Historical Society of Pennsylvania, Letter dated October 22, 1794 from Joseph Cowperthwait to Thomas Mifflin.

(110) Slaughter, pp. 205-209; Microfilm M986 Reel 1, United States vs. William Bonham, United States vs. James Quigley et al., United States vs. John Queen et al.

(111) Jonathan Forman 1755-1809, *Incorrect Journal of Our March into Pennsylvania,* Darlington Memorial Library, University of Pittsburgh; C. P. Humrich, Esq., "The Relations Which the People of Cumberland and Franklin Counties Bore to the Whiskey Insurrection of 1794," Kittochtinny Historical Society Papers Vol. 3, 1903, p. 230; Slaughter, p. 217; Letter, Alexander Hamilton to Thomas Mifflin, October 10,1794, Manuscript Collection of the Rosenbach Museum and Library; Gerald Carson, "A Tax on Whiskey? Never!" *American Heritage*, August 1963, p. 104; Interview with Vaughn Whisker, August 7, 1990.

(112) John C. Fitzpatrick, ed., *The Diaries of George Washington, 1748-1799,* Vol. IV (Boston: Houghton Mifflin Co., 1925), pp. 212-216; Syrett, Vol. XII, p. 540; Letter William Findley to William Bradford, September 16, 1794, Manuscript Collection of the Historical Society of Pennsylvania.

(113) Letter, George Washington to William Augustine Washington, September 28, 1794, Manuscript Collection of the Rosenbach Museum and Library; A. J. Dallas, Letters of the Western Insurrection, Book 2, Carlisle, October 13, 1794, Manuscript Collection of the Historical Society of Pennsylvania; Tagg, p. 208.

(114) Slaughter, pp. 79-88; Letter, George Washington to James Ross, Esq. August 6, 1794, Germantown, Manuscript Collection of Rosenbach Museum and Library.

(115) Linn and Egle, pp. 411-415, 416-419; Dumas Malone, ed., *Dictionary of American Biography*, Vol. VI (New York: Chas. Scribner's Sons, 1961), pp. 107-108; Don Yoder, *The Picture Bible of Ludwig Denig: A Pennsylvania German Emblem Book,* Vol. 1 (New York: Hudson Hills Press, 1990), p. 26; Jeanne A. Calhoun," 'Light Horse Harry' Lee and the Whiskey Rebellion, " paper read at Old St. Lake's Church, September 24, 1993.

(116) A. J. Dallas, Letters of the Western Insurrection, Book 2, Carlisle, October 4, 1794, Bedford, October 23, 1794, Cherry's Mill, October 31, 1794.

(117) Adams, pp. 140-141; *Annals of Congress,* U.S. Debates and Proceedings of Congress, 4th-5th Congress, Albert Gallatin on Direct Taxes, pp. 1837-1838.

(118) Baldwin, pp. 244-246; Slaughter, p. 218; McClure, pp. 653-654; Letter, Charles Smith to Jasper Yeates, Pittsburgh, November 13, 1794, Historical Society of Pennsylvania Miscellaneous Collection.

(119) N. Leroy Baldwin, *Two Hundred Years in Shade Township, Somerset County, Pennsylvania 1762-1962* (Central City: N. Leroy Baldwin, 1964), p. 62; Joseph F. Rishel, *Founding Families of Pittsburgh: The Evolution of a Regional Elite, 1760-1910* (Pittsburgh: University of Pittsburgh Press, 1990), p. 27.

(120) Leland Baldwin, p. 258; Slaughter, p. 219.

(121) Linn and Egle, pp. 460-466, 479-480.

(122) Microfilm M986 Reel 1, United States vs. William Peterkin

(123) Stephen B. Presser, "A Tale of Two Judges: Richard Peters, Samuel Chase, and the Broken Promise of Federalist Jurisprudence," *Northern University Law Review*, Vol 73, 1978-79, p. 81; *Journal of Dr. Christian Boerster, 1785-1833,* Somerset Historical Center, p. 37.

(124) Presser, p. 81; Linn and Egle, p. 472.

(125) Presser, p. 82.

(126) Presser, p. 75.

(127) A. J. Dallas, Letters of the Western Insurrection, Book 2, Bedford, October 23, 1794, Manuscript Collection of the Historical Society of Pennsylvania.

(128) Brackenridge, pp. 19-21; Pennsylvania State Archives, Harrisburg, RG-4, *Records of the Office of the Controller General, Western Expedition (Whiskey Rebellion) Accounts, 1794-1804; Journal of Dr. Christian Boerster,* p. 36; Robert Porter Trial Transcript.

(129) Tagg, p. 214; Carson, p. 105.

(130) Betts, p. xvi; Letter Tench Coxe, Commissioner of the Revenue, to Thomas Marshall, Esq., Supervisor of the Revenue, Buckpond, Kentucky, March 30, 1797, original in the possession of Jane Wood Wise.

Map of the Seven-County Whiskey Rebellion Study Area

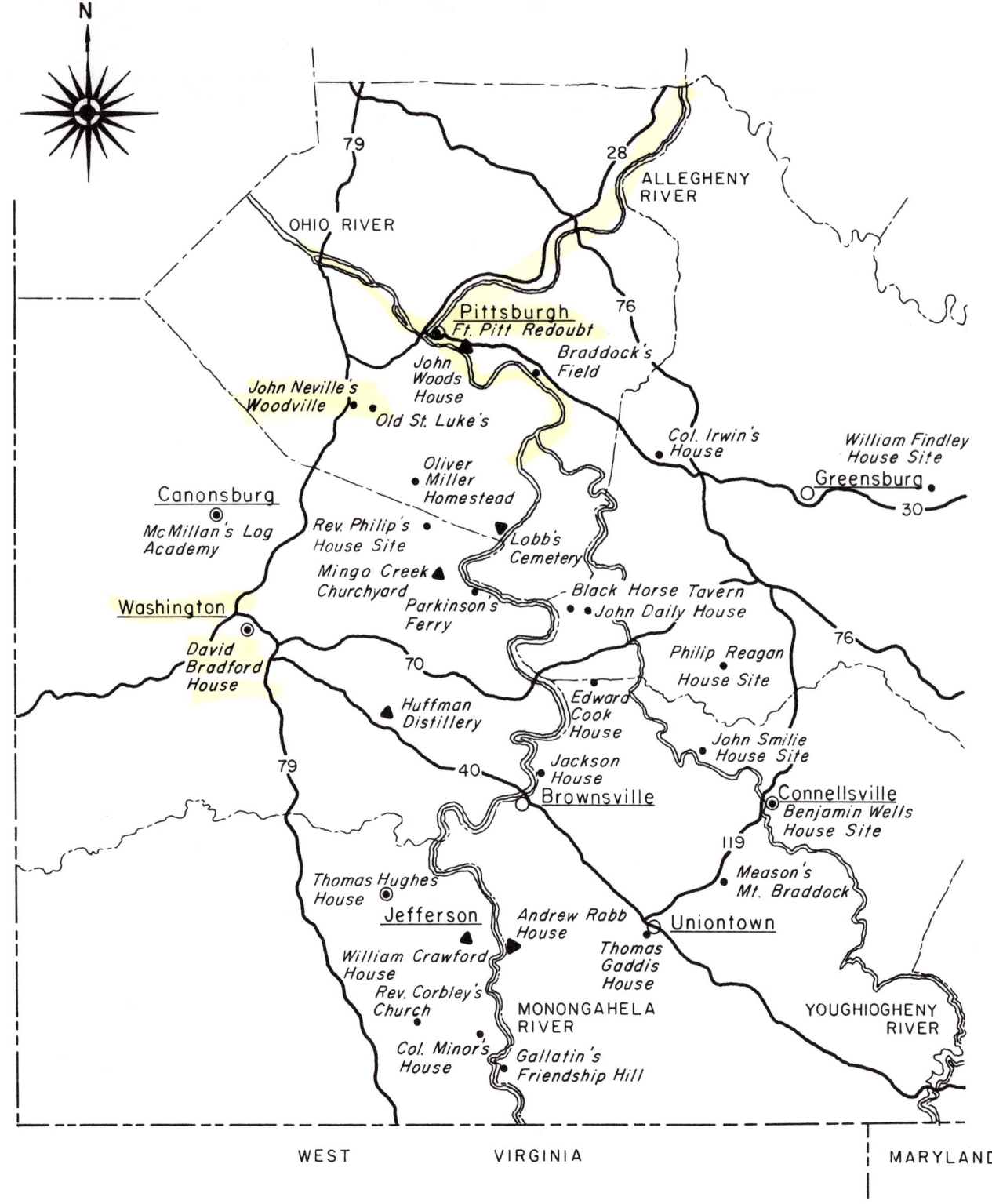

This section shows Allegheny, Greene, Washington and parts of Fayette and Westmoreland counties.

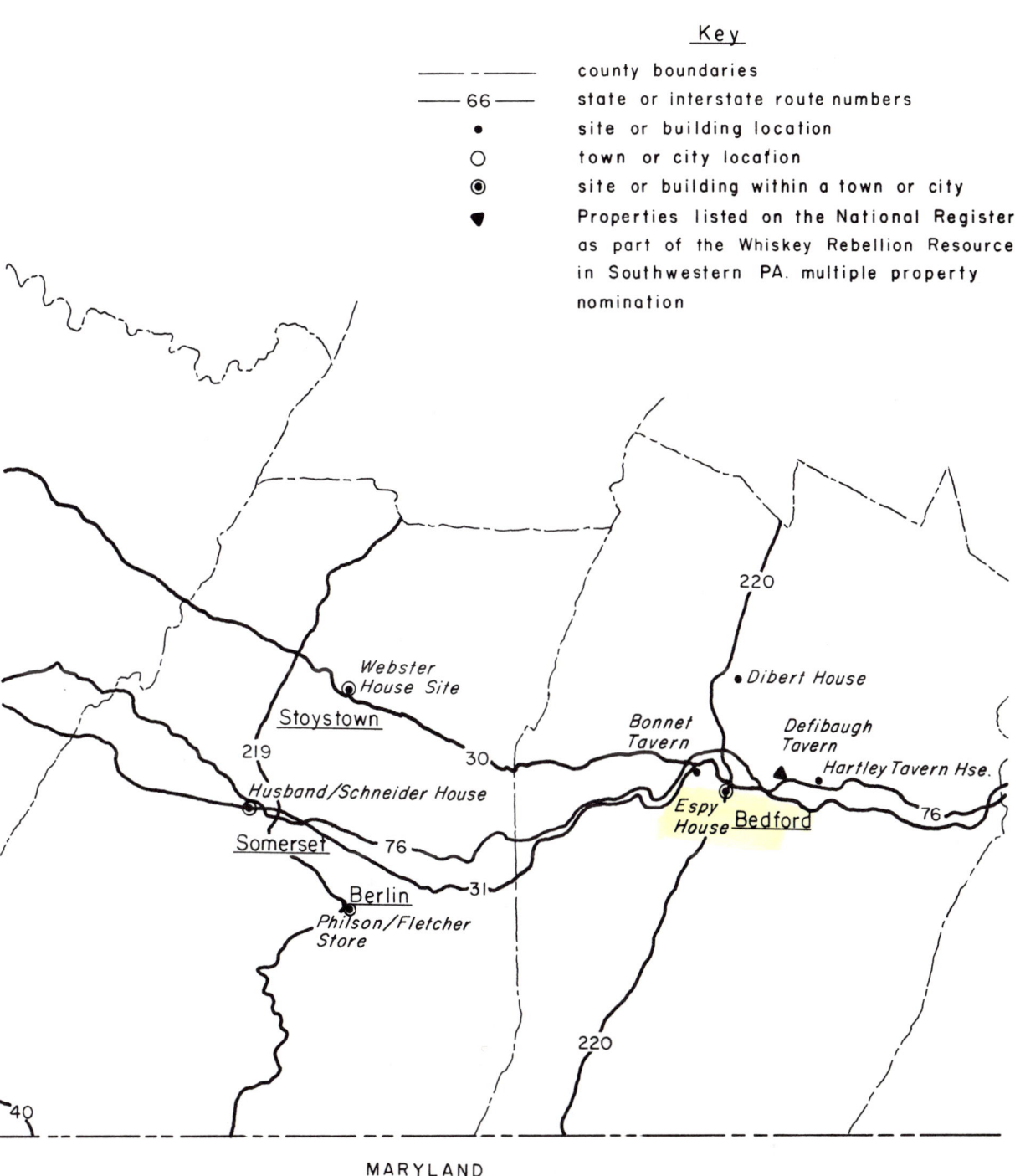

This section shows Bedford and Somerset counties and part of Westmoreland County.

Regional Guide

Guide to Associated Sites and Remaining Buildings Within the Seven County Region

This section of the book is intended to provide a guide to the buildings and sites which have been documented to be associated with the Rebellion, as well as to those whose relationship could not be documented. Although some of the latter were pointed out by local historians, their significance in association with the Whiskey Rebellion could not always be proven, or their documentation indicated that they did not date to that period. However, all have been included here to show the whole range of sites associated with the Rebellion, from those little known or seemingly insignificant to those of state and national importance, and from those known only through oral history to those documented in manuscripts and histories.

One benefit of touring the actual sites is that it provides the contemporary traveler the chance to experience the topography of the region as well as discover the regional spread of the sites and their relationship to each other. It also may provide an opportunity for those interested in the region's history to see how fragile their historic resources are. The built environment of western Pennsylvania has drastically changed in two hundred years. Most of the buildings, structures, and sites associated with the Rebellion have been obliterated through decay and demolition. Traveling to the sites not only helps the historian imagine the hardships of the late eighteenth century, when travel was by foot or horseback, it also helps him or her conceive of the determination and perseverance these political activists exhibited in carrying out their convictions. It also illustrates the relationship the early transportation routes had to their primary focus, the rivers of the region. In addition, traveling to the various sites makes one aware of the relationships the communities of the region had with their meetinghouses or churches, and gives one a sense of how and where the leaders of local government lived. The writer has developed a kind of kinship with some of the Whiskey Rebellion personalities through traveling to where they lived, worked, worshiped, and are buried.

The guide is broken down into the seven counties where research and survey work were done for this Whiskey Rebellion study. Research was initiated using primary and secondary resources, not only to determine the scope of architecture to be found in the region, for the period covered by the study, but also to learn who were the significant persons associated with the Rebellion in each county. Members of the Whiskey Rebellion Bicentennial Task Force Steering Committee were consulted to learn of local historians and sites within each of the counties. Site visits were then conducted to evaluate extant buildings and sites, as well as to visit local archives and interview local historians. Part of the purpose of this study was to determine what remained of the built environment representing the Whiskey

Rebellion era and the people associated with it.

Since most of southwestern Pennsylvania was a frontier in the early 1790s, many of the political, religious, and economic leaders lived in relatively modest houses. It was only after the Rebellion, in the late 1790s and the early 1800s, when the threat of Indians was gone, transportation systems were developed, and the commerce of the area had blossomed, that men of means built large, well-appointed houses. Most of the houses that can be associated with Whiskey Rebellion figures were built in this latter period.

In 1984 three properties in the region were designated as part of a Whiskey Rebellion National Historic Landmark study: the **Espy House** in Bedford, the **Neville House** in Allegheny County, and the **Bradford House** in Washington. (National Historic Landmark designation means the property has national significance and retains integrity from its period of historic significance.) These will be described at different points during the following narrative. Fifteen properties have been listed on the National Register of Historic Places in association with the Whiskey Rebellion. (The National Register of Historic Places is the federal government's list of properties that are significant in local, state, or national history, architecture, or archaeology.) Most have little documentation on their Whiskey Rebellion association, and some of this information is erroneous. This has been largely corrected through documentation in the historic context of my 1992 Whiskey Rebellion multiple property nomination as well as through added information to some of those nominations. The writer has attempted to make this research more inclusive by the involvement of local historians and incorporation of their perspectives as much as possible.

In all, seventeen properties not previously surveyed or nominated were identified as associated with people or events of the Whiskey Rebellion. These included ten houses, three taverns, a log academy building, a log distillery, and two cemeteries. Considering that there were thousands involved in the Whiskey Rebellion, and that the names of a few hundred men can be found consistently in government reports, contemporary accounts, histories, and Court of Quarter Session records, this number is indeed small. Of these seventeen properties, seven were determined to be eligible for the National Register and were included in a multiple property National Register nomination titled, "Whiskey Rebellion Resources in Southwestern Pennsylvania."

Context of Early Architecture in Southwestern Pennsylvania

Generally, the earliest buildings of southwestern Pennsylvania were constructed of logs. Log construction was best adapted to frontier living as it was relatively simple in form and economical in construction in terms of materials and time. Research indicates that the men who participated in the excise protest were, on the average, small farmers, mechanics, and laborers, many of whom were landless. These people lived in small wooden or log buildings, typically of only one room. Few, if any, of these structures survive from that period. None could definitely be traced to the rebels. What has survived are the homes of the upper or upper middle class of the period—the economic and political leaders on both sides of the excise issue. Such leaders generally had more significant and better-documented roles during the Whiskey Rebellion. The **Thomas Gaddis House** south of Uniontown and the **William Crawford House** southeast of Carmichaels are examples of larger log houses that have survived, although precariously, from that period.

There were some notable exceptions to this, however. Certain areas of Fayette County had a higher than usual ratio of stone houses. Early examples of these include the previously mentioned **Edward Cook House** in Washington Township and the **Andrew Rabb House** in German Township. Both are believed to have been built in the 1770s. Both Cook and Rabb became large landholders/entrepreneurs and proclaimed their success on the frontier through a powerful architecture of substance and solid craftsmanship. Brick houses were not built generally until after 1800. However, Albert Gallatin, a large landholder in southern Fayette County, chose to build his 26 x 29 foot house of brick in 1789. According to architectural historian Charles Stotz, stone was the choice building material from the late eighteenth century through the early nineteenth, but by 1830 brick buildings were overwhelmingly in evidence throughout the region.(1)

To document the kind of housing found in southwestern Pennsylvania during the era of this study, statistics have been extracted from the 1798 Direct Tax. This tax assessed houses and outbuildings according to size, material, age, number of windows, and, apparently, sometimes workmanship. The variations in information found in this record depended on the assessor. A tabulation of these records shows that eighty-eight percent of the highest valued houses of the region were built of logs. Just over five percent were built of stone and less than one percent were built of brick. Actually, the percentage of stone houses may have been even smaller because the majority of dwelling houses of the region were appraised at less than $100, and the building materials for these were not specified. In addition, since log or wood construction was the cheapest construction form in terms of materials and labor, the inhabitants of low or middling income would have lived in small buildings of this type. The average size, figured from a sampling of western Pennsylvania houses in 1798, indicates they were of one- or two-room plans.(2)

By 1798 the town of Pittsburgh had already established a preference for a building material distinct from that of the surrounding countryside. Here, twenty-seven percent of the finest buildings were constructed of brick, only two percent were of stone, and the remainder (seventy-one percent) were frame or log. This preference for brick is similar to that of other established Pennsylvania towns and cities, such as Lancaster and Philadelphia.

Vernacular architecture historian Karen Koegler has found stone houses clustered in the older settled townships, those containing the county seat, and areas near the Monongahela River. This would correspond with social historian R. Eugene Harper's study in which he found the river townships the most advanced. Redstone Township in Fayette County had eighteen percent of its finest houses built of stone, the highest percentage in the region. It was the elites of the region, no matter their ethnic background or area of origin, who built the stone houses. However, some noted politicians remained in small log buildings in 1798, living in a manner close to the people they represented. Among these were William Findley of Westmoreland County and John Smilie of Fayette County. On the other hand, politician Hugh Brackenridge lived in a two-story frame house in Pittsburgh, valued at twice that of his rival John Woods's stone house and six times that of the frame **Neville House** (Woodville), then in St. Clair Township. Men of means such as Isaac Meason, Albert Gallatin, and Edward Cook chose prominent hilltop positions to locate their stone and brick houses.(3)

Although Koegler found the three-bay, side-hall plan the most common house plan, my studies of Whiskey Rebellion-related properties show a variety of bays and plans. I have found houses ranging from two bays to seven bays, with side halls, central halls, and variants of the hall/parlor plan. In fact, there is a wide variety of forms found in the region. The greater part of these houses were constructed with plans that show some ethnic influence or retain earlier vernacular features, but that also display the ever-increasing influence of the Georgian plan. (The Scotch-Irish had a perceptibly larger impact on the vernacular housing of southwestern Pennsylvania than of southeastern Pennsylvania. In addition, the average dwelling value in the western part of the state was only a fraction of that in the East.) A Georgian house in its purest form is recognizable by its five-bay facade. Each bay is evenly spaced, and the external expression is one of symmetry. In these houses there is a central passage, and each room is designed with a specific function in mind. In earlier building traditions, such as the hall/parlor plan, entry into the house was directly into the hall, an inclusive term which denoted both kitchen and living space. This hall/parlor served as the social center of the house. In addition, in these earlier building forms, rooms were multi-functional.(4)

In conclusion, the late eighteenth/early nineteenth-century vernacular architecture of southwestern Pennsylvania was not only changing and evolving in response to the traditional building styles of the various ethnic groups in the region, but was also influenced by the popularization and demands of the Georgian plan and the Federal style of architecture.

Bedford County

Although Bedford County was not in the heart of the protest area, in September 1794, U.S. Peace Commissioners Jasper Yeates and William Bradford reported to Secretary Hamilton that

> *the disaffection seems to have spread in Bedford County; where about ten days ago near two hundred men assembled and in the very view of the Court which was then sitting erected a liberty pole (with a six striped flag) which is still standing and bears the inscription that is the common one among the Insurgents.*(5)

Local historians have tended to see Bedford County's role in the Rebellion as the location where the federal troops converged, where

Washington reviewed the troops, and the point furthest west to which Washington accompanied the troops. Bedford is important as the site where the left division, consisting of troops from Maryland and Virginia, assembled with those of the right division from New Jersey and Pennsylvania, but it is important to know that the excise protest was being voiced here too. Washington saw the area just west of Bedford town as the beginning of rebel territory and gave instructions to General Lee how to proceed from there. One of the federal soldiers wrote to his father on October 19, 1794,

> *Last evening we came to this place, Bedford, a little town situated in the forks of the Juniata, the town is small and consists chiefly of log houses. We are now almost in the midst of the insurgents— not one of them dares to shew his head, many of them have fled, and there is not the smallest appearance or account of their making the least head or opposition against us.(6)*

Front elevation of the Espy House, Pitt Street, Bedford.

Histories of Bedford County note that Washington lodged at the **Espy House** during his stay in Bedford. This two-and-one-half-story, three-bay, stone house is situated on the main street (123 Pitt St.) of Bedford. It is a two-thirds Georgian style house with the hall/stairway extending along the western side of the house. Washington had his headquarters in the large room stretching across the entire front of the second floor. The building is now the home of the Washington Bakery.

The fact that 125 men were charged with inciting a riot or treasonous proceedings in 1794 not only indicates the high degree of protest activity in Bedford County, but also may indicate the degree of pressure from the federal government to prosecute men on what now seem minor offenses. Local histories indicate that some of these men were involved in raising a liberty pole at the **Bonnet Tavern** four miles west of Bedford. Located at the intersection of present-day Routes 30 and 31, the **Bonnet Tavern** was placed on the National Register for Historic Places in 1979. A Pennsylvania Historical and Museum Commission historical marker was dedicated there in May 1992 to commemorate the activities there of whiskey rebels and the encampment of the federal army on their march west.

Just as taverns served as gathering places for patriots during the American Revolution, they played an essential role during the Whiskey Rebellion as well. It was here that local farmers and artisans could not only discuss events within their communities, but also learn from travelers of events outside of their communities. Taverns such as the **Bonnet Tavern** also served as rendezvous points for excise protest groups. There are two other taverns in Bedford County associated with the Whiskey Rebellion, the **Defibaugh Tavern** and the **Hartley Tavern/House**. Both are located along U.S. Route 30, which was known as the Pennsylvania Road during the 1790s.

Built c.1785 in what was then Providence Township, the **Defibaugh Tavern** is a good example of a vernacular style, log tavern/ house. The eastern section of this two-and-one-half-story banked building is the original part of this rare surviving example of late eighteenth-century taverns in western Pennsylvania. Typical of period vernacular style taverns, the **Defibaugh Tavern** was built with multi-tiered porches and was extended over the years with additions of various sizes. A door on the east gable end opened into the barroom. (In what is now known as Snake Spring Valley Township, the tavern is about three miles east of Bedford.)

The Defibaugh family played a locally significant role in whiskey distilling and whiskey retailing during the Rebellion. Jacob and Adam Defibaugh, sons of Casper Defibaugh, were charged with treasonous activities during the summer and fall of 1794 in association with the whiskey excise protest movement. Adam was charged with riot, assault and battery in the August Quarter Sessions Court of Bedford County. In all probability it was at that time that the "liberty pole" was erected in sight of the courthouse. Jacob was a farmer/distiller, and his brother John Gottlieb was a tavernkeeper.

Although the two-and-one-half-story, four-bay, stone **Hartley Tavern/House** was apparently built soon after 1798, it was noted by local historians for its association with the Whiskey Rebellion. William Hartley was a large landowner, distiller, and innkeeper. After his death in 1798, his wife Susanna continued the tavern business. According to local histories, Mrs. Hartley entertained George Washington with games of backgammon at her house on his return east from Bedford.(7) (Also located in Snake Spring Valley Township, the Hartley property is about five and a half miles east of Bedford.)

Jacob Naugle was also among those named in the Bedford County Quarter Sessions for excise protest in 1794. What is perhaps the only intact building associated with him is located south of Bedford and just north of the Bedford Springs Hotel. However, this could not be documented in court records. This one-and-one-half-story, two-bay dovetailed log building is situated across the road from the stone gristmill there and is part of the Bedford Springs Hotel National Register Historic District.

The south and east elevations of the "Jean Bonnet Tavern," located at the fork of Routes 30 and 31.

Some of the rebels mentioned in the Quarter Session accounts can be traced to Bedford Township, where the first of the rebels were arrested (George Wisegarver and George Lucas). Local historian/ genealogist Glenna Fisher pointed out the locations of their homesteads on Dunnings Creek north of Bedford. Among these is the **Frederick Dibert House**. According to oral tradition, the cellar of the house became a whiskey storehouse when the report came that the federal troops had arrived in Bedford. Scott Dibert, the present owner of the property, said that seventy-four barrels of whiskey were stored there. (The doors were wide enough to roll the barrels in.) The present two-and-one-half-story, three-bay, plank and frame bank house was reportedly built in 1795 by Michael Dibert for his son Frederick.(8) (This property is located north of Bedford on Dibert Road at Dutch Corner.)

Somerset County

There was a center of excise protest in the area around Berlin, Somerset County, which was predominantly settled by Germans.

This appears to counter the general impression given by some historians that only the Scotch-Irish were involved. However, the most widely mentioned Berlin rebel is Robert Philson (1759-1831), a native of Ireland. He was one of four Bedford County rebels taken to Philadelphia for trial. (Somerset County was created out of the western part of Bedford County in 1795.) Philson was charged with treason for attending the Parkinson's Ferry meeting in August, 1794, which was more precisely termed, "traitorously assembled to raise and levy war on the United States." Philson was also involved in writing letters to others across the state encouraging them to participate in the protest. He was acquitted in 1795 and in the same year was elected to the state legislature. He continued to be politically active in later life, serving as associate judge, and in 1821-22 representing his district in Congress.(9)

Dr. Christian Boerster wrote in his journal that when he arrived in Berlin in August 1794, everything was in an uproar on account of the new excise law. When the federal troops arrived in Berlin in October 1794, Governor Mifflin established his headquarters in Boerster's home. Boerster was subsequently a witness at Philson's trial. A notation dated October 21 1794, from Boerster's journal reads, "In the evening [went] to Bedford and appeared before Judge Mr. Peters and State's Attorney and was sworn a witness, in order to report what we knew against Robert Filtzen [Philson] and Hermann Hossband [Husband] in respect to the insubordination against the excise and the state."(10)

The Philson-Fletcher Store on the square in Berlin, Somerset County.

The only extant resource associated with Philson is the **Philson-Fletcher Store/House** situated on the corner of Diamond and Main streets (501 Main St.) in the square of Berlin. (John Fletcher was the uncle of Philson, and they were partners in a mercantile operation from the late eighteenth century into the early nineteenth century.) This greatly altered, two-and-one-half-story, four-bay log store/house is the location, according to local histories, where Philson raised a liberty pole.

An incident on June 27, 1794, confirms the heated debate concerning the excise tax in Berlin. On that day Frederick Long, Nicholas Lysenberger, Jacob Barnd, Christian Evli, and Salomi Zimmerman entered the schoolhouse in Berlin and committed a "riot rout on the body of John Gunsinghouser," the schoolmaster. The case was taken to the August Quarter Sessions Court of Bedford County. This is the only known case where a woman was publicly involved in a Whiskey Rebellion-related incident. Robert Philson put up some of the bail money for one of the defendants.(11)

Berlin is located in Brothers Valley Township, which had the highest number of Somerset County men brought before the Bedford County Court in 1795 for treasonous activities. This township was early settled by German Baptists, or Brethren, who bestowed the name upon the settlement. The Brethren, at their Annual Meeting in Somerset County in 1789, were counseled to "put their distilleries away" in order to promote peace and tranquillity among the members. Nevertheless, many did not heed these words, and eleven Baptists were among those indicted for nonpayment of the tax. One of the worst things that could have happened to a member of that church was to be brought to civil court for unlawful conduct. Among this group of eleven was one elder, two sons of elders, and the son of a deacon. The church excommunicated all of them, and only one made restitution for his acts and was restored to membership in the church.(12)

Religious and political pamphleteer Herman [Hormon] Husband (1724-1795) was another resident of the region that became Somerset County and was actively involved in the excise protest. He saw these issues as being most pertinent to westerners in 1794: access to western lands, accountability of elected officials, and the process of amending laws. His writings alarmed tax collectors Benjamin Wells and Philip Reagan, and after they fled to Philadelphia, they effectively impressed United States Commissioner of Revenue Tench Coxe with their anxieties. Consequently, Husband was labeled a dangerous man and was arrested and taken to Philadelphia for trial.(13)

Husband owned several tracts of land in and around what would become Somerset Borough. The only extant building associated with Husband is located at 555 East Main Street in Somerset. He purchased the property in 1782 and, according to tradition, built the two-and-one-half-story, two-thirds Georgian style log house, now covered with weatherboards. Two additional bays were added in the early nineteenth century by the next owner, Adam Schneider, and the whole house appears to have been remodeled about the mid-nineteenth century in the Greek Revival style. Schneider was assessed in 1798 with a one-and-one-half-story house of hewed logs measuring 26 x 30 feet. Consequently, although the **Husband/Schneider House** has become well known in the twentieth century for its association with Husband, little if any of the present structure was there at the time of Husband's ownership.

The east elevation of the Husband/Schneider house, Main Street, Somerset.

John Webster, tavernkeeper and excise collector for Bedford County, had his home and office at Stoney Creek in Quemahoning Township (just southeast of Stoystown) during the Rebellion. According to Congressman William Findley, Webster was not well liked by many of the poor residents of Bedford County. Findley stated,

Webster made a practice of seizing liquors on the road from poor people, who were carrying it to procure their salt, or other necessaries; sometimes he was contented with receiving the excise tax and letting the liquors pass, but generally he kept all, and sometimes detained the horses for a time, restoring them again as a matter of favour.

In the summer of 1794 a company of about 150 men marched from Westmoreland and Bedford counties to his house, demanded his commission, and made him promise never to collect the excise again. Fire was set to his haystacks and stables, but the more moderate party was the majority. They extinguished the fire and protected Webster from every injury other than insulting language. After promising not to act as collector again, he was released.(14)

On August 2, 1794, Webster wrote to General Neville in Philadelphia, "Benjamin Wells house and barns are a pile of ruins, I expect every night I lay down that I shall have to arise with mine all in fire about my head." In the same letter he seems to regret that any stillers he has turned in may be fined, except "Old Mr. Wisegarver, he has been violent against the law." This explains why George Wisecarver was among the first four arrested and taken to Philadelphia.(15)

Webster, like other excise collectors, fled to Philadelphia at the height of the insurrection, and returned with the federal army. Quickly retracting his promise not to collect the tax, Webster in December 1794 requested a small company of light horse to be stationed in the county so that the law "would be attended with a more immediate compliance." Still somewhat fearful, he engaged a young man to ride a few days with him while registering stills in the lower part of the county.(16)

Webster's letters to Neville portray a greedy man who was quick to seize a still or whatever else he could if the distiller did not follow the letter of the law. Even at the death of his wife in June 1795, his foremost concern was that her illness had prevented his "attending to stamping my stills."(17) In July 1795 Webster moved from Stoney Creek to Stoystown, where he had built a new house. It is believed that the current Deaner Funeral Home (on old Route 30) is the site of that house. An inspection of the basement revealed walls and timbers from an earlier building.

Fayette County

Research of primary and secondary sources reveals that Fayette County men played key roles on both sides of the excise issue. Men such as Colonel Edward Cook and Albert Gallatin were prominent in the political gatherings at numerous locations.

Cook was elected chairman of four excise protest meetings. Although opposed to the excise, he did not advocate violence. He was a delegate to the first Pittsburgh meeting in September 1791 and was elected chairman of that meeting. He was apparently chosen not only because he was highly respected in the community but also because he was not a radical. This group of moderates sought to work peacefully to change what they believed to be an unfair law. They were concerned for their financial interests as well as their liberties. Not only was Cook chairman of various excise protest meetings but also of the militia committees at the Braddock's Field rendezvous.(18)

Because of his conspicuous position, Cook was among those excepted from the general amnesty proclaimed by General Lee. However, nothing was found against him, and he was never arrested. When the federal troops marched through the area, some of them nearly demolished his distillery, knocking in the heads of the liquor casks, and spilling a vast amount of whiskey. Cook died in November 1808. The epitaph on his tombstone at Rehobeth Cemetery reads in part,

> *Few men have deserved and possessed more eminently than Colonel Cook the confidence and esteem of the people of the Western Country, in public spirit, disinterestedness, and zeal for the general welfare he was excelled by none...(19)*

Cook migrated to the area that became Fayette County in 1770. By the 1780s Cook was the county's wealthiest citizen, and his prosperity continued into the 1790s. Simultaneous with his expanding economic interests was his rise as a community and civic leader. His two-and-one-half-story, four-bay stone house, built in the 1770s in Washington Township, is probably the most intact house associated with the Whiskey Rebellion. (Located south of Route 70, the house is reached by taking Exit 21 [Arnold City exit] and proceeding onto Rehobeth and Cook Roads, one-and-a-half miles south.) In fact, considering Cook's significant role in the Rebellion and the high degree of integrity of the **Cook House**, the property should be considered part of the Whiskey Rebellion National Historic Landmark nomination. The **Cook House** was placed on the National Register for Historic Places in 1978.

The c.1773 Edward Cook house, showing the asymmetrical fenestration of its facade, Washington Township, Fayette County.

Albert Gallatin, an early entrepreneur and political economist, first bought land in Fayette County in 1786. By the 1790s he had become a leading spokesman for the democratic beliefs prized on the American frontier. He played a key role in moderating the Whiskey Rebellion. His speeches at Parkinson's Ferry and Brownsville were particularly effective in breaking the power of the insurrectionary faction of the rebels.

The first section of Gallatin's house was built of brick in 1789. This two-and-one-half-story, three-bay house was not particularly large for the period. A frame addition was added sometime before 1798. Directly east and at right angles to the original sections, a two-and-one-half-story, three-bay stone addition was completed in 1823. At this time the brick and frame sections were stuccoed to blend with the addition. The stone addition was designed and built by Scotch-Irishman Hugh Graham. He is one of the few known architect/builders in early southwestern Pennsylvania besides Adam Wilson, who designed Isaac Meason's mansion. Gallatin was not pleased with Graham's finished product. He disparagingly labeled it a "Hyberno-teutonic style." He said the exterior had the appearance of an "Irish barracks" while the interior finishes were similar to those of a "Dutch tavern."(20) Gallatin's **Friendship Hill** was designated a National Historic Landmark in 1965. The property became part of the National Park system in 1979. **Friendship Hill** was renovated 1990-92 and dedicated in November 1992. (To reach the site take Route 119 south from Uniontown to Point Marion or take Route 166 south from Masontown to New Geneva.)

Fayette County's locally prominent men (those generally known only within the county's borders), such as Robert Ross, Andrew Rabb, and Thomas Gaddis, were actively involved against the excise while Benjamin Wells served as a focus for anti-excise sentiments. Revolutionary War veteran Robert Ross was a large landholder and a locally important militia leader of German Township. He led a group of 145 rebels to Uniontown to erect a liberty pole there. He escaped capture by federal troops until a general amnesty was granted to all offenders. In 1798 he was assessed with two houses. Although local historians indicated that one of Ross's houses stood east of Masontown, research of Fayette County deeds proved that the Ross family only owned it from the late nineteenth century.

Andrew Rabb (c.1740-1804) was a wealthy and prominent distiller who lived in German Township. Reportedly he had a secret formula which produced a greater return from the amount of grain used. During the early stages of excise protest, Rabb was accused of threatening violence on excise collector Wells, but later he tried to moderate the protest and restore peace to the region. He was fairly typical in that he was against the excise because of the adverse effect on his business, but at the same time he was against violence which might result in the loss of his property. He was a justice of the peace and a militia officer. As a civic and commercial leader, his actions and reactions to the excise tax were fairly typical of the upper class in southwestern Pennsylvania. Rabb's five-bay, two-and-one-half-story stone house was built in the vernacular Georgian style in 1773. This is confirmed by a signature and date inscribed in the plaster of the western gable wall of the attic. The **Rabb House** represents only a handful of houses that have survived from that period in the southwestern Pennsylvania region.(21) (The Rabb property is located about a mile and a half north of Masontown off Route 166.)

The north elevation of the c.1773 Andrew Rabb house, German Township, Fayette County.

Like Andrew Rabb, Thomas Gaddis was among the political and propertied elite of Fayette County. He was a colonel in the militia and an early settler of Union Township. He was involved early in the excise protest, being one of those who met at Pittsburgh in August 1792. Gaddis was one of only two men from Fayette County arrested and taken to Philadelphia to prison. He was charged with treason for "traitorously assembling" at Uniontown on August 10, 1794. State Representative Albert Gallatin stated in a letter that Gaddis was accused of setting a pole in Uniontown. At his trial in May 1795, a verdict of "ignoramus" was found on the count of treason. (The ignoramus verdict indicates that the jury did not receive sufficient information to indict Gaddis on that charge.) However, he was found guilty on the charge of misdemeanor for raising the liberty pole. Jonathan Rowland's deposition given April 22, 1795, for the trial gives insight into this liberty pole raising. On the day of the raising, the inhabitants of Fayette County were requested to meet four miles from Uniontown. Gaddis went to see what it was all about. He met several hundred men on their march to town and consequently appeared to be their leader. A yoke of oxen was pulling the pole behind them. Rowland quoted Gaddis as saying that the boys were determined to go to town to set up a liberty pole, and it was not in his power to dissuade them. Gaddis did request that the people be civil "to affront no man or his property."(22)

Although termed a "settler's fort," the **Thomas Gaddis Homestead** was evidently erected as a house upon this tract, c. 1769-74. The present structure on the site is a highly deteriorated three-bay, one-and-one-half-story log building resting on a low rubblestone foundation. It is not only a rare survivor as a small log house but also as a house with rare diamond-notched corner timbering. The **Gaddis Homestead** was placed on the National Register for Historic Places in 1974. (Located in South Union Township, the Gaddis homestead is about two miles south of Uniontown off old Route 119.)

Excise collector Wells was notoriously unpopular. His house near Connellsville was attacked twice in 1793. However, he persisted in collecting, and in 1794 it was burned to the ground. After his house was burned, he moved across the Youghiogheny from the area formerly known as New Haven to Connellsville, where he opened the first store in 1794. Wells evidently found tax collecting to be a lucrative operation. In 1800 he wrote to Supervisor Neville indicating he would like to be involved in the collection of the direct tax which had been enacted in 1798. According to records of that tax, he had built a stone house on Water Street measuring 30 x 26 feet, the highest-valued building in Bullskin Township. The site of Wells's house is near the Crawford School on North Seventh Street in Connellsville.(23)

A 1974 view of the Thomas Gaddis House with the Chestnut Ridge in the background, South Union Township, Fayette County.

Of all the counties of southwestern Pennsylvania, it was in Fayette County that population, land use, and agriculture first developed to the point where nascent industries could develop. A small class of wealthy individuals had begun to launch business enterprises there by the 1790s. Among this class of wealthy men was entrepreneur Isaac Meason. In 1791 he built the Union Furnace on Dunbar Creek, believed to be the second iron furnace constructed west of the Alleghenies. When unrest and violence became widespread during the summer of 1794, it was men of means such as Meason who came under attack, as well as the excise officers. Thus, some of the rebels met during Meason's fair at Dunbar and erected a liberty pole at Union Furnace, which was in full blast at the time. At a height of ten feet a board was attached upon which was written, "Liberty and No Excise."(24)

Meason's formal announcement to the world of his wealth and stature was the construction of his mansion, built in 1802 between Uniontown and Connellsville, now in Dunbar Township. Called Mt. Braddock, this Georgian style stone mansion was built according to the Palladian plan. Designed by Scotch-Irish architect-builder Adam Wilson, it is a premier example of its type in America, and continues to dominate the immediate landscape of the area. This property was designated a National Historic Landmark in June 1990. (Located in Dunbar Township, the Meason House stands just east of Route 119 about five and a half miles north of Uniontown.)

Another Fayette County pioneering industrial entrepreneur was Samuel Jackson. In 1777 Jackson (1750-1818) settled where the Redstone Creek meets the Monongahela River. Not only did he erect a sawmill, gristmill, and smith shop on his property, he was also instrumental in establishing the first paper mill west of the Alleghenies, which he built upstream from his other enterprises. Just before his death, he began construction of the Albany Glass Works, which was continued by his sons. A member of the Society of Friends and opposed to the distillation of liquors, Jackson favored the government tax as a means of suppression of what he considered a vice. He had unabashedly dubbed the Parkinson's Ferry meeting a "scrub congress," and armed men from Washington County sought his punishment. Consequently, he was brought before the Brownsville meeting later that same month, which Hugh Brackenridge attempted to mollify on his behalf. The rebels dismissed him with the appellation of a "scrub Quaker" and a fine of a round of whiskey for all. According to Dr. Wellford's diary, the Fredericksburg Cavalry were

The front elevation of the c.1785 Samuel Jackson house, Jefferson Township, Fayette County.

stationed at Jackson's mill. Wellford himself stayed at Jackson's house one night, but did not like his reception there and evidently suspected his loyalty to the federal government.(25)

Histories indicate that Jackson constructed the stone house, which still stands near Albany in Jefferson Township, in 1785. The 1798 federal tax lists him with a two-story stone house 40 x 20 feet, a stone kitchen measuring 19 x 22 feet, a stone mill, a hay house and stable, and a sawmill. The **Jackson House** is a two-and-one-half-story, five-bay, stuccoed stone house with a kitchen ell to the rear. The first floor of the main block consists of a central hall with a parlor on either side. (The Jackson House is located on the north side of Route 201 about a mile northwest of Brownsville.)(26)

Men of means such as Meason, Gallatin, Cook, Jackson, and Rabb, who were among the wealthiest men within their respective townships, built substantial houses which remain standing. In addition, the less substantial Gaddis log house survives as well. Consequently, Fayette County, of the counties surveyed, has the most documented extant buildings associated with the Whiskey Rebellion.

Westmoreland County

Westmoreland County, although having centers of excise unrest, including the area around Greensburg in Hempfield Township and the southwestern townships bordering Fayette and Washington counties, appears to have, of any county surveyed, the fewest tangible resources remaining to represent the Whiskey Rebellion era. Records indicate that excise rebels generally lived in small wooden structures and survey records show that these did not survive well; this is especially true in Westmoreland.

There is nothing to represent even the county's best-known personage from the era, William Findley. Findley was an antifederalist congressman who wrote his personal account of the Rebellion soon afterward in 1796. Not only was he concerned that an accurate record of the Rebellion be preserved, he also wanted to rectify what had already been written by his political opponents, Hugh Brackenridge and Treasury Secretary Hamilton. After learning that he had been misinformed on certain things, he attempted to revise his account, but the revisions were lost on the way to the printer. Findley lived in Unity Township, where in 1798 he was assessed with a two-story wooden house measuring 26 x 24 feet and a kitchen measuring 18 x 18 feet. Helping to shape political opinion in this region, he lived modestly in solidarity with the common people, who were his constituents. He met and spoke with them on their own grounds, and accordingly, he was repeatedly elected to represent them. According to Albert's *History of Westmoreland County*, written in 1882, his house was located on the site of the Monastery Coke Works and had recently burned down.(27) (The site of Findley's house is about a mile northeast of St. Vincent College near the corporation boundary of Latrobe.)

Rostraver Township, Westmoreland County, located between the Youghiogheny and Monongahela rivers, was in the heart of the excise protest region. It is bounded by Fayette County to the south, Allegheny County to the north, and Washington County to the west. The township has several buildings and sites tenuously associated with the Rebellion. Among these is the **John Daily House**. A mill owner, distiller, and storekeeper, John Daily was apparently involved in the protest and was bound over for trial at York by Judge Addison on November 14, 1794. His two-and-one-half-story, five-bay brick house near Webster was evidently built soon after 1798, for the federal tax of that year lists him with a one-and-one-half-story log and frame house. Architectural historian Charles Stotz evidently considered the **Daily House** one of the most finely detailed Federal style houses in southwestern Pennsylvania. His book devoted four pages of photos and drawings to this house.(28) (The Daily House is located between the north and south bound lanes of Route 51 about four miles north of Route 70.)

Another property within this township and just northwest of the **Daily House**, with relevance to the Whiskey Rebellion, is the **Black Horse Tavern**. This tavern was kept by Revolutionary War officer Gabriel Peterson in 1794. Located about midway on the great road leading from Budd's Ferry on the Youghiogheny River to McFarlane's Ferry on the Monongahela River, the **Black Horse Tavern** served as a rendezvous for whiskey rebels, according to local tradition. The present two-and-one-half-story, three-bay brick house in the vernacular style was apparently built by tavernkeeper William Sampson between 1798 and 1808. (The tavern is located less than a half-mile northwest of the Daily House on the west side of Route 51, where it meets Salem Church/Webster Roads.)

View of the east and south elevations of the Black Horse Tavern, Rostraver Township, Westmoreland County.

Two churches within the township were related to the Rebellion. **Salem Baptist Church** was one of those served by Rev. David Philips, who was active in the protest. Although this church was organized in 1792, the present stone building wasn't erected until 1842. Built in the traditional meetinghouse form, this one-and-one-half-story brick church has a three-bay gable-fronted facade. This church is situated on one of the high-topped hills, which provides a panoramic view of the rolling landscape of this region. The land for the church was donated by early settler Joseph Budd, who also established Budd's Ferry on the Youghiogheny. (Salem Church is located about a mile and a half northeast of Route 51 on Salem Church Road.) The other is **Fell's Church**, located almost directly south of the **Daily House**. Built in 1834, this two-and-one-half-story, stone church replaced a log church built there in 1792. Like the **Salem Church**, **Fell's Church** has a three-bay gable-fronted facade with doors at each side. The land for this Methodist church was donated by Benjamin Fell. An early settler of Rostraver, Fell was locally prominent in its religious and civic affairs and signed the amnesty in September, 1794. Captain Matthew Beazel, who also signed the amnesty, is buried there.(29) (Fell's Church is about three miles north of Route 70 and a half mile west of Route 51.)

Another extant Westmoreland County property which has some relevance to the Whiskey Rebellion is **Brush Hill**, the mansion built by Colonel John Irwin. Irwin was an associate judge of the county and a representative in the General Assembly. He was called upon by Hugh Brackenridge to help quiet the mob during the incident at

A 1950 view of John Irwin's c.1798 "Brush Hill," Irwin Borough, Westmoreland County.

Drumm's Hotel. The two-and-one-half-story, seven-bay stone house appears to have been built in 1798, as the federal tax for that year lists Irwin with a house not finished measuring 34 x 54 feet. It was probably one of the largest houses west of the Alleghenies at that time. At Irwin's death the property passed to his son-in-law John Scull, founding editor of *The Pittsburgh Gazette*. Although a staunch Federalist, Scull was intimidated by excise protesters to print articles and advertisements written by the rebels. Scull's newspaper served as a major pipeline of information on what was occurring in the western counties during the Rebellion. Irwin's **Brush Hill** was placed on the National Register for Historic Places in 1975. (This property is located on Brush Hill Road about half a mile north of Route 30 in Irwin.)

Although 150 men from Westmoreland County allegedly attacked excise collector John Webster in Bedford County, the much smaller forces of men who attacked the peace commissioners at Drumm's hotel in Greensburg and excise collector Philip Reagan's property in South Huntingdon Township were the ones which produced records of indictments and names of those involved. Therefore, it may appear there were fewer participants than actually was the case. In addition, no local historians were found who could direct the writer to possible lesser-known historic sites and properties, as was done in previous counties.

Allegheny County

The actions and reactions regarding the excise tax in Allegheny County show the real dichotomy of feelings within the region. On one side were the landed rich, such as the Nevilles and Craigs in the Chartiers Valley south of Pittsburgh, and the rising mercantile class of Pittsburgh who favored the excise. On the other side, the small farmer and laboring classes were opposed to it. Having John Neville, along with his political faction of ardent Federalists, within the county served to polarize the area and resulted in the worst violence of the region.

Allegheny County, with its convergence of rivers, early attracted settlers, and its commercial success along with convenient natural resources promoted industrial growth. This and the parallel urbanization of the county have led to the almost complete obliteration of eighteenth-century houses and structures. Therefore, besides the **Neville House** at Woodville, the **Walker-Ewing House** in Collier Township, the **Woods House** in the Hazelwood section of Pittsburgh, and the **Brick Redoubt** of Ft. Pitt, little of the built environment associated with the Whiskey Rebellion in Allegheny County remains.

An 1872 print showing the Fort Pitt Redoubt. Note the gambrel roof of Isaac Craig's house in the background.

The **Fort Pitt Redoubt**, now in Point State Park, was used by Supervisor Neville as an excise office and as such is probably the only extant tax collection point. Neville's son-in-law Major Isaac Craig used it as a residence. The one-story, five-sided stone, log, and brick building was built in 1764 by Colonel Henry Bouquet. This unusual five-sided structure has been greatly altered over the years. In the 1830s Russell Smith made a painting of the blockhouse, when it served as part of the residence of local official/entrepreneur Isaac Craig. Mary Schenley, granddaughter of contractor/financier James

O'Hara, gave it to the Daughters of the American Revolution in 1894. A restoration of dubious authenticity, conducted by the DAR, occurred between that date and 1902. Fleming's *Scenes of Old Pittsburgh* depicts the structure in various stages of transformation. An 1840 print shows the datestone on another elevation of the building just under the eaves, rather than above the arched doorway, its current position. All other doors and windows shown in nineteenth-century views of the building have been infilled with brick and stone. The **Ft. Pitt Blockhouse** is listed on the National Register as part of the Forks of the Ohio nomination.(30)

Isaac Walker of Robinson Township was charged with treason for being at Braddock's Field. The c.1790 **Walker-Ewing House**, in present-day Collier Township, was given by Isaac to his daughter married to Alexander Ewing. This two-and-one-half-story, two-bay, v-notched log house was placed on the National Register for Historic Places in 1976 and is currently owned by the Pittsburgh History and Landmarks Foundation. A relatively small house (26 x 20 feet), it has a gable-end door. (The Walker-Ewing House is located about three miles south of the Carnegie exit of Interstate Route 79 South on Noblestown Road.)

View of the c.1790 Walker-Ewing house from Noblestown Road, Collier Township, Allegheny County.

The **Oliver Miller House** in South Park, although the site of the original log house, was not built until after the Rebellion. The present two-and-one-half-story, four-bay, stone house was built in two sections—one was constructed in 1808, the other in 1830. The property is nevertheless important as the site where the sparks of the Rebellion were ignited. (This property was listed on the National Register in 1975.) It was at the nearby farm of William Miller that U.S. Marshal Lennox and Inspector Neville first encountered the ire of whiskey rebels. The area was much torn by the excise issue. A neighbor of the Millers, James Kiddoe, complied with the excise law and had his barn burned and gristmill partially destroyed by rebels. (The Miller House is located about a mile southwest of Route 88 between Castle Shannon and Library, on the corner of Corrigan and Stone Manse drives.)

In addition to the **Miller Homestead**, there are at least two sites within the county, **Braddock's Field** and **Bower Hill**, which may be noted for their distinction during the Whiskey Rebellion. **Braddock's Field** was the site of the largest armed resistance to government from the time of the Revolution to the Civil War. It appears much information has been collected on the site as to the location of Braddock's defeat, but little in association with the Whiskey Rebellion. Most of the meeting area on the Monongahela flood plain has been covered over with industrial growth and encroached upon by the continual urbanization of the Monongahela Valley during the nineteenth and twentieth centuries. Although there is an area on the bluff known as the "Battlefield Wilderness Remnant," which has not been developed, what open space actually remains consists largely of two cemeteries and an abandoned strip mine. (Much of the actual battleground is located just north of Braddock Avenue in Braddock Borough, but the remnant is in North Braddock Borough.)

The Neville home at **Bower Hill** was the site of the most destructive and most deadly engagement during the Rebellion. This apparently recently built mansion symbolized the wealth and power of eastern mercantile interests. As the inventory account indicated, the house was "neatly finished, painting and papering complete, done in the best manner, with the best materials—[there was] carpeting over the whole house, rooms, passage and stairs." While the majority of farmers living on the frontier endured primitive living conditions in a one- or two-room cabin valued at less than $100, Neville was dwelling in relative splendor in a house appraised at $2,400.(31)

Local historian Canon Richard Davies of Old Saint Luke's Episcopal Church guided me to the approximate site of **Bower Hill**. We walked the area which is now grass and parking lots between Kane Memorial Hospital and Our Lady of Grace Catholic Church, trying to find a more exact location. According to a 1936 Pittsburgh *Post Gazette* article, a one-and-one-half-story frame house with Italianate elements was built over the site of the original mansion. The 1889 *History of Allegheny County* confirmed that the **Wrenshall House** was built on the site of the Neville mansion.(32)

The key Federalist supporter in the West was John Neville. A Revolutionary War officer, he was appointed Inspector of Revenue for the western counties by President Washington. Up until that time Neville had been a popular figure among his countrymen. Although one account notes that he contributed to the relief of suffering settlers, his correspondence with his tax collectors and his business transactions indicate the excise tax continued to increase his monetary gains after the Rebellion. The inscription from his tombstone reads:

> *During his long life he filled many important offices both Civil and Military; in the former, he was virtuous and disinterested, In the latter, he was patriotic and brave. He enjoyed the friendship and confidence of the illustrious Washington. The day of his death witnessed the most pleasing tribute that can be paid to the Memory of a Mortal, the Sincere regrets of his Friends and the tears of the neighboring poor.(33)*

The **Neville House** (**Woodville**) had been turned over to his son Presley by the time of the Whiskey Rebellion. According to some sources, after Neville's mansion house was burned at **Bower Hill** the family took refuge at **Woodville** for a time. This conflicts with Hugh Brackenridge's account, which places Robert Johnson, the deputy excise collector, at this house during this period. (Johnson had been involved in the excise conflict from the beginning. He was the first collector attacked in 1791 near Pigeon Creek.) According to tradition, at one time there was a direct view from **Woodville** to **Bower Hill**. **Woodville** is part of the 1984 Whiskey Rebellion National Historic Landmark nomination.(34) (**Woodville** is located on Washington Avenue [Pennsylvania Route 50] just off the Heidelberg/Kirwan Heights exit of Interstate Route 79.)

Anne Genter and Betsy Martin led me through the c.1785 **Neville House**. This one-and-a-half-story, five-bay frame house is currently being restored by its owners, the Pittsburgh History and Landmarks Foundation. The exact date of construction of the house is unknown, but it is believed the log kitchen wing was the first building there. The main house was originally four bays, but the fifth bay was added to

A c.1916 view of the Wrenshall house on the site of Neville's Bower Hill. Evidently it was used as a basis for the Iams print, "Counsel Before the Attack." See p. 46.

the west gable end to connect the main house with the kitchen.

Mentioned earlier, **Old St. Luke's Church** was established by the Neville and Craig families. The present stone, Gothic Revival style building, constructed in 1852 on the site of the earlier church, is located about a half mile northeast of **Woodville** on Washington Pike.

Another locally important meeting place for whiskey rebels was **Couch's Fort**. This was a local rendezvous for people during Indian attacks and was located on Nathaniel Couch's tract of land. At the time of the Rebellion it was part of St. Clair Township. The fort was actually a dwelling that was subsequently demolished. The site is now in Bethel Park Borough near the intersection of Route 19 South and Ft. Couch Road and is occupied by a McDonald's restaurant.

John Woods (1758-1816), a well-to-do political leader and member of a prominent founding family of Pittsburgh, played a locally significant role in the Whiskey Rebellion. As part of the Neville connection, a group of socially and politically prominent residents of the Pittsburgh area, he is representative of the Federalist leanings of Pittsburgh, the commercial heart of southwestern Pennsylvania in 1794. A political opponent of Hugh Brackenridge, Woods initiated rumors against him during Secretary Hamilton's investigation of those involved in the Rebellion. The c.1792 **John Woods House** is significant as a rare surviving example of a late eighteenth-century vernacular style house in Pittsburgh. Located at 4604 Monongahela Avenue in the Hazelwood section of Pittsburgh, this two-and-one-half-story, three-bay stone house is banked into the bluff rising above the Monongahela River. The property has been listed on the National Register as part of the Whiskey Rebellion Resources in Southwestern Pennsylvania multiple property nomination.(35)

A 1970s view of the c.1792 John Woods house in the Hazelwood section of Pittsburgh.

The **Lobb's Cemetery and Yohogania County Courthouse Site**, situated in Jefferson Borough, is significant for its association with the late eighteenth-century regional governmental and judicial center located there. Although Virginia relinquished its claim to southwestern Pennsylvania in 1780, this area continued as an area of political unrest into the 1790s, when the Whiskey Rebellion broke out. Because the federal government recognized it as a pivotal area, troops were ordered stationed there to maintain peace in the region. The camp was swept by smallpox, which resulted in the death of several men. Two Virginia officers, who died in January 1795, are buried there. Another Whiskey Rebellion figure buried there is Andrew McFarlane (1751-1829), possibly twin brother to James McFarlane, who was killed at Bower Hill. Andrew was a highly visible participant of the Mingo Creek meeting and the Braddock's Field muster. Geographically a center of the region's political unrest, **Lobb's Cemetery and Yohogania County Courthouse Site** is the only known burial ground of federal troops who died during the western expedition of 1794. This property was listed on the National Register in 1992 as part of the multiple property nomination of that year. (**Lobb's Cemetery** is located northeast of Calamity Hollow Road and west of Pennsylvania Route 837.)

Washington County

Washington County in 1790 had a population double that of Allegheny County and included present-day Greene County. The county seat of Washington was thriving with only about sixty fewer people than Pittsburgh. The county contributed some of the key players in the excise protest movement. Two particularly active areas were the Mingo Creek/Parkinson's Ferry area and the town of Washington. Both Mingo Creek and Washington were the location of either a militia association or a Democratic Society, two of only three such organizations in western Pennsylvania. These extralegal groups functioned to oversee and chastise sitting officeholders, and propose a slate of candidates for local offices. They were one of the reasons the county received the wrath of President Washington.

Washington County, on the edge of the Pennsylvania frontier, had all of the ingredients to be at the center of the Whiskey Rebellion: ardent law-and-order Federalists; Republican/antifederalists, who believed strongly in the right to protest, particularly the right to protest against an unfair tax; active militias, including the militia-run Mingo Creek Association or Society; strong religious leaders on both sides of the issue; both a number of very wealthy people and some very poor people; and young and ambitious politicians who had quickly risen to power on the frontier.

When the excise tax was first enacted, not only were the upper- and lower-class people of the county generally opposed to it but the political and religious leaders as well. However, talk of violent protest, war, and secession polarized the people. Religious leaders such as Rev. John McMillan made it clear that they would not tolerate any breaking of the law. Political leaders such as Judge Alexander Addison, Judge James Edgar, and lawyer David Redick contributed at different levels and in different situations to return law and order to the region. On the other hand, political and military leaders such as David Bradford and Benjamin Parkinson chose to take the excise protest movement from words and written petition to military action. Bradford was at the top of Washington's list of those to be arrested and brought to Philadelphia, and it was no accident that Washington directed General Lee to march the army with Parkinson's Ferry in view as its destination.

The **Mingo Creek Presbyterian Churchyard** contains the graves of some of the region's prominent whiskey rebels. Most notable is the grave of James McFarlane, who led the second march on the Neville house at **Bower Hill**. Others involved in the whiskey excise protest buried there include John Hamilton (1754-1837), David Hamilton, Benjamin Parkinson (1763-1851), John Holcroft, and John Gaston.

Mingo Creek Church and Churchyard, as the political, social, and cultural center of its community, acted as a nerve center for the region during the Whiskey Rebellion. Not only did the church members congregate here, but militia groups and the "Mingo Creek Society" as well. Research showed that Nottingham Township, which contained **Mingo Creek Church** in the late eighteenth century, was the residence of about half the most active Whiskey Rebellion

View of the Mingo Creek Churchyard with David Hamilton's stone in the foreground and the 1831 Mingo Creek Presbyterian Church in the background.

participants of Washington County. Mingo Creek and nearby Parkinson's Ferry were the locations of two important excise meetings during the summer of 1794.

The Mingo Creek Society, or Hamilton's District Society, was attended frequently by as many as three hundred persons. Both Findley and Brackenridge dubbed the region the "cradle of the insurrection." This area was also home to Hamilton's battalion of militia. It was named for the commanding officer, Colonel John Hamilton, who was also sheriff of Washington County at the time of the Rebellion. Dorothy Fennell in her study of the Whiskey Rebellion found that most of the participants in the Rebellion were militiamen. The fact that ordinary men were armed and organized militarily contributed greatly to the ease with which opposition moved to rebellion. Hamilton's battalion was at a militia hearing when news arrived that the United States Marshal was "carrying people off to Philadelphia." Thus began the chain of events that led to the death of McFarlane and the burning of Bower Hill.(36)

Located just east of Fromans Run and Route 88, the present one-and-one-half-story brick church at Mingo Creek was built in 1831. Built in traditional meetinghouse form, Mingo Creek Church's six-bay gable front faces onto Mingo Creek Road. The oldest portion of the graveyard is on the steeply rising hill south of Mingo Creek Road, which runs between the church and churchyard. The earliest tombstones date to the 1790s, with Whiskey Rebellion martyr James McFarlane being the earliest adult burial. The church and churchyard were placed on the National Register in November 1992 as part of the multiple property nomination.

A member of Mingo Presbyterian Church and a local historian, Gilbert Balliard, led me to the site of John Holcroft's house in Nottingham Township, now Union Township. Although historians cannot be certain, Holcroft is credited with coining the name Tom the Tinker, and this became his alias. Holcroft's well-crafted will indicates that he was more than an unthinking political agitator. He was appointed assessor of Nottingham Township for the 1798 federal direct tax. Although he was taxed for a log house at that time, the site of his house is now occupied by a two-and-one-half-story, three-bay stone house built in 1832. This vernacular Federal style house was built by Thomas and Elizabeth Storer, and its first floor displays a variation in the two-thirds Georgian plan. Elizabeth was one of Holcroft's younger children. Located about a mile and a half east of Gastonville near Gilmore Road, this property was listed on the National Register as the **Dusmal House** in 1975.

Revolutionary War veteran John Gaston (1740-1823) lived at Finleyville in Peters Township, a short distance from the Holcroft site. It is not known if Gaston was coerced into delivering the "Tom the Tinker" letter to *The Pittsburgh Gazette* in September 1794, but in November 1794 he was bound for appearance at the next Quarter Sessions Court for Allegheny and Washington counties for actions concerning the Whiskey Rebellion. Located on the eastern edge of Gastonville, the **Gaston House** is a five-bay, two-and-one-half-story brick house with an asymmetrical facade. Although the unevenly spaced windows and the off-center chimney make it appear that the house may have been built in two sections, the brick masonry work indicates that this was the original design. This c.1812 vernacular style house is unusual in that there are two entrances, one into the main hall at the western end of the house, and one into the kitchen at the eastern end of the house. The main doorway and cornice show elements of the Federal style.

Balliard also led me to the locations of the David Hamilton houses at Ginger Hill. A justice of the peace and distiller, David Hamilton (1759-1839) was an active participant in the Rebellion. (In addition to his previously mentioned cousin John, his brother Daniel Hamilton also was involved in the Rebellion.) As earlier mentioned, David's home was the polling place for the district, and the Mingo Creek Society or Association was also known as Hamilton's District Society. He was closely associated with David Bradford, and historian Leland Baldwin portrays him as among those who influenced Bradford into becoming the leader of the radical rebel faction. On the other hand, Brackenridge's writings indicate that Hamilton also tried to prevent violence whenever possible. Active in the Mingo Creek Presbyterian Church, he willed one-half his estate "to assist poor and pious young men who may be educated with a view to the Gospel Ministry." In 1798 David was assessed for a two-and-one-half-story stone house, the only stone house and one of the highest-valued houses in Nottingham Township. Research indicates that the only remaining house that may be associated with him stands southwest of Ginger Hill. It is a two-and-one-half-story, five-bay, single-pile frame house with a one-and-one-half-story stone ell to the rear.(37) Located at the intersection Route 917 South and Route 136 East in Carroll Township, the vernacular style **Hamilton House** appears to have been built in the early nineteenth century.

Other buildings that appear to have been part of this tract were torn down c.1925-26. These stood in what is now the parking lot of Ginger Hill School. They were a series of three, southerly facing, connected log buildings which sloped down the hill to the east. The one nearest the road on the west was two stories while the others were one story. The two-story building had a large fireplace on the first floor, and it was here according to tradition that Hamilton entertained the excise officers late one rainy evening after he had spiked their whiskey with Jamaican ginger. While the intoxicated officers slept, Hamilton's stills were removed and hidden. This is how the area became known as "Ginger Hill."(38)

Another house surveyed was that of David Bradford located at 175 South Main Street in Washington. The **Bradford House** is a four-bay, two-and-one-half-story stone house built in 1788 according to the two-thirds Georgian plan, or with a side hall and two parlors on the first floor. The first stone house built in Washington, it was considered a mansion at the time of its construction. The fireplace surrounds and overmantels were executed in the Adamesque style. An impressive feature of the house is the mahogany staircase which extends from the first floor to the third. In 1798, it was still the only two-story stone house in Washington and the second-highest-valued property in town. A part of the 1984 Whiskey Rebellion Historic Landmark nomination, the Bradford House was purchased in 1959 by

View of the Federal style facade of the 1788 David Bradford house, Main Street, Washington.

the Pennsylvania Historical and Museum Commission, who restored it in 1963.

A religious figure whose influence transcended the region's politics was Rev. John McMillan. His influence was so great in the region that Hugh Brackenridge referred to him as "Cardinal McMillan." McMillan is said to have known no fear or favor. McMillan came to the region in 1775 and settled in Strabane Township. About 1785 he established an academy in a small log building on his farm. It became Canonsburg Academy in 1791 and later developed into Jefferson College. In 1895 this one-and-one-half-story, two-bay log building was moved to Canonsburg. This fourteen-foot-square, v-notched log building is a rare survivor of a building typical of the frontier period in southwestern Pennsylvania. The **McMillian Academy** is now located on College Avenue on the campus of the Canonsburg Junior High School.(39)

View of the log cabin McMillan Academy, Canonsburg.

Although the writer surveyed distillery sites and ruins in Fayette, Westmoreland, and Washington counties, only two remain intact, and both of these are in Washington County. The **Huffman Distillery and Chopping Mill** is located in Somerset Township. The c.1790 distillery building is an essentially square, one-and-one-half-story, v-notched log structure which rests on a rubblestone foundation. All of the building's structural members are hewn, including the common rafters. The first-floor log section is plastered, both inside and out. Besides the low, squat door and a window above it in the east gable end, there is only one other opening on this floor. The plaster and general lack of fenestration seem to indicate that this floor was used for storage. The eaves ends of the structure's ground level have opposing doors as well as opposing squat windows. These were to allow for plenty of ventilation. Typically, this is where the actual distilling occurred.(40)

View of the south and east elevations of the log and stone Huffman Distillery, Somerset Township, Washington County.

Associated with the distillery is a c.1805 timber-frame chopping mill. Although it appears to be a small barn from the exterior, this building was used to chop and grind the grain for the distilling operation. As with most vernacular commercial/industrial buildings, the building's size and shape were largely dictated by the source of power. In this instance, it was a horse-powered treadmill operation. There was a ramp located at the northwest corner of the building which was used by the horses to enter the treading area. Inside along the western wall, the floor upon which the horses would have trodden is composed of thick planks sawn on an up-and-down sawmill. There is a circular niche in the northern wall necessitated by the large wooden wheel, a vital part of the pulley system of the horse-powered mechanism. This timber-frame building has three bents of massive posts and beams and is sheathed with vertical boards.

The **Huffman Distillery and Chopping Mill** are significant as rare surviving examples of late eighteenth/early nineteenth-century buildings associated with this once flourishing industry in southwestern Pennsylvania. In addition, these buildings typify the small scale of industrial/commercial enterprises of that period. They were listed on the National Register in November 1992 as part of the multiple property nomination. This property is located off LR62155 about a mile and a half north of Cokeburg and two miles north of State Route 917.

Greene County

Few names of rebels were found for the area which became Greene County. Of those mentioned, Rev. John Corbley's was the most widely known. A Baptist minister, he was arrested and taken to Philadelphia despite the fact that he had not been a major actor in the actual rebellion. Noted as a very effective preacher, Corbley was an ardent patriot and preached political freedom as the counterpart of an untrammeled liberty of conscience. Men like Corbley were arrested to be used as examples whose trial and execution for treason would deter other disaffected citizens from plotting rebellion. In May 1782 Corbley's family was massacred near Garard's Fort by a small band of Indians. Corbley, deep in meditation, was following a distance behind his young family on their way to church early one Sunday morning. His wife, baby, and two small children were killed and scalped. Two other daughters were scalped but survived. Corbley himself was unhurt, but this was probably the most trying experience of his life. Corbley's experience with the Indians went to the heart of the issue created by the charge that the central government was impotent in dealing with frontier problems, yet demanded internal taxes. Similarly, other frontiersmen lived in fear of Indian attacks. It was obvious to these people that they should be exempt from additional burdens, especially federal taxes.(41)

View of the east elevation of the c.1800 John Corbley house, Greene Township, Greene County.

Local historian Rev. Roland Cadle led me to Corbley's two-and-one-half-story, five-bay brick house less than a mile north of Garards Fort on LR30027 in Greene Township. Although the facade is symmetrical, there are, instead of a central door, doors on either side of a central window. Evidently, the floor plan is a variation of the hall/parlor plan, with a central room serving as the hall/parlor. According to genealogist Nannie Fordyce, religious meetings were held in this large central room. Although a 1984 National Register nomination and a commemorative plaque on the front of the **Corbley House** state that it was built in 1796, the 1798 federal tax notes Corbley with a house measuring 25 x 30 feet (probably of logs, according to its value), a barn, and a milk house on three hundred acres. Corbley's will indicates that he was a very large landholder, having tracts in Pennsylvania, Virginia and Kentucky.(42)

Corbley was among those arrested by Captain Dunlap's Company on November 13, 1794, a night known as the "Dreadful Night." Imprisoned in Philadelphia in December, he was detained until March 15 without a hearing, but was allowed the privilege of the city. When he was paroled, he returned to Greene County on foot and returned likewise in May for his trial.(43)

The Federalist government saw men like Corbley—highly visible and vocal men—as threats to the order of the nation. Therefore, they sought to silence them on charges which now appear unsubstantiated. Men like Corbley saw themselves as defending the same rights, those of free speech and assembly, that had been fought for almost twenty years earlier. Corbley's friend John Minor was also punished for siding with the whiskey rebels. Although Minor was appointed an associate justice when the new county was erected in 1796, Federalist Alexander Addison, president judge of the Western Pennsylvania

Judicial District, had him put out of office. (44)

Thomas Hughes (1749-1823) was another early settler of Greene County who became involved in the whiskey excise protest. He was charged with being among those with blackened faces who attacked the house of Captain Faulkner in 1792. Faulkner had opened his house in Washington for excise collection. A locally prominent landowner and distiller, Hughes was also charged with having signed a "contemptuous and improper paper" in September 1794. He was among the twenty-three men excepted from Governor Lee's pardon. His home is located on Hatfield Street, on the northern boundary of Jefferson Borough, the town which he laid out. (During the 1790s this land was part of Cumberland Township.) The present two-and-one-half-story, three-bay stone bank house on the property was built in 1814. A cantilevered one-and-one-half-story, two-bay kitchen addition is located on the southern gable end. This house also has two front doors, the central one opening into the front parlor and the other into the hallway. The **Hughes House** was purchased by the Pennsylvania Historical and Museum Commission in 1967 and was listed on the National Register for Historic Places in 1972.(45)

Another locally prominent Cumberland Township resident was Colonel William Crawford (1744-1826). As a well-to-do political and military leader, he played a locally significant role in the Whiskey Rebellion. Public figures such as Crawford played key roles, not only in protesting the tax, but in moderating the protest to prevent violence as well. An early settler of southern Washington County, which later became Greene County, Crawford was a justice of the peace and a Revolutionary War patriot. Crawford represented Cumberland Township at the Parkinson's Ferry meeting. Cumberland Township had the largest number of stills and the second-highest number of distillers within Washington County. Naturally, the excise tax was important to these people.

Crawford was charged with treason for being at Braddock's Field. He was taken prisoner along with his son by Captain Dunlap in November 1794. After several months imprisonment in Philadelphia, he was released on bail. According to trial records, Crawford was charged with being "traitorously assembled" in Pitt Township, Allegheny County, on August 1, 1794. (This was the date of the rendezvous of western militias at Braddock's Field.) At his trial for treason on May 11, 1795, he was absolved of any wrongdoing, his verdict being "ignoramus."(46)

Built c.1815, the **William Crawford House** stands one and a half miles southeast of Carmichaels, off Brown's Ferry Road and Stevenson's Lane, as an unusually well-preserved vernacular log house from the early settlement period in Greene County. This full-dovetailed log house was covered with horizontal siding sometime in the late nineteenth or early twentieth century. The two-and-one-half-story, three-bay **Crawford House** has the general appearance of symmetry, but the front door is slightly off center. The house was built in the hall/parlor plan with the front door opening into the hall. Cumberland Township was one of the areas which appeared intransigent to the federal government, and William Crawford, as a locally prominent civil and military leader in Washington/Greene County and

View of the west elevation of the c.1815 weatherboarded log William Crawford house.

as a representative of Cumberland Township, became a logical target for arrest and imprisonment by the federal government in the fall of 1794.

Another Greene Township resident and participant in the Whiskey Rebellion was John Badolet. A native Swiss and the lifelong friend of Albert Gallatin, Badolet attended the excise meeting at Pittsburgh in 1792 and was a township representative at the August 1794 Parkinson's Ferry meeting. Badolet owned three lots in Greensboro and by 1798 was assessed with a one-story frame house measuring 25 x 15 feet. Local historians had felt his house might still be standing in Greensboro. However, the suggested building was a log cabin, measuring 26 x 22 feet, and was moved from the banks of the Monongahela River in 1990 to a new location in Greensboro. (47)

In Greene County, as in previously studied counties, those who were singled out and arrested by the federal government were the civil, militia, or religious leaders of long-standing influence in their respective communities. No residents of Greene County could be considered regional leaders in the excise protest, but all had their local sphere of influence. Greene County, with the largest amount of land yet to be settled, best portrayed some of the issues confronting American citizens living on the frontier, including the need for military protection, the opening of free trade routes, and their perceived right to protest won by their participation in the American Revolution.

Notes

(1) Charles M. Stotz, *The Architectural Heritage of Early Western Pennsylvania* (Pittsburgh: University of Pittsburgh Press, 1936), p. 26.

(2) These tax statistics were compiled from two townships from each of the seven counties of this study. The townships chosen were those most closely related to Whiskey Rebellion activities.

(3) Karen Koegler, "Building in Stone in Southwestern Pennsylvania: Patterns and Process," Paper presented at the 1990 Vernacular Architecture Forum, Lexington, Kentucky; Robert Eugene Harper, "The Class Structure of Western Pennsylvania in the Late 18th Century" (Ph.D. dissertation for the University of Pittsburgh, 1969), pp. 19, 42.

(4) Henry Glassie, *Pattern in the Material Folk Culture of the Eastern United States* (Philadelphia: University of Pennsylvania Press, 1968), pp. 48-55; Nancy Van Dolsen, *Cumberland County: An Architectural Survey* (Ephrata, Pa.: Science Press, 1990), pp. 1-24; Catherine W. Bishir, *North Carolina Architecture* (Chapel Hill: University of North Carolina Press, 1990), pp. 9-12; Charles Stotz Photograph Collection, Carnegie Library, Pittsburgh; Lee Soltow, *Distribution of Wealth and Income in the United States in 1798* (Pittsburgh: University of Pittsburgh Press, 1989), p. 77.

(5) Pennsylvania Whiskey Rebellion Collection, Letter Jasper Yeates and William Bradford to Secretary Alexander Hamilton, September 5, 1794.

(6) Letter Nathaniel Boileau to his father Isaac Boileau, MSS Collection of Ulysses Grant Miller Library, Washington and Jefferson College.

(7) E. Howard Blackburn, *History of Bedford and Somerset Counties, Pennsylvania*, Vol. I (New York/Chicago: Lewis Publishing Co., 1906), p. 481.

(8) Conversation with Glenna Fisher, August 6, 1990; conversation with Scott Dibert, August 7, 1990.

(9) *The Papers of Albert Gallatin*, microfilm (Philadelphia: Rhistoric Publications, 1969) sponsored by New York University and the National Historical Publications and Records Commission; Microfilm M986 Reel 1, *Criminal Case Files of the U.S. Circuit Court for the Eastern District of Pennsylvania, 1791-1840*, Roll 1, Case Files, 1791-1799.

(10) *Journal of Dr. Christian Boerster 1785-1833*, MSS Collection of Somerset Historical Center, pp. 34-35, 69-70.

(11) Adam Miller, Esq., "Toket" 1791-1798, Berlin Historical Society, pp. 58-59.

(12) H. Austin Cooper, *Two Centuries of Brothersvalley Church of the Brethren 1762-1962* (Westminster, Md.: The Times, Inc., 1962), pp. 132-138.

(13) Dorothy E. Fennell, "From Rebelliousness to Insurrection: A Social History of the Whiskey Rebellion, 1765-1802" (Ph.D. Dissertation for the University of Pittsburgh, 1981), p. 193; Herman Husband signed his name as "Hormon" in his will, written November 9, 1789 and probated August 20, 1795.

(14) William Findley, *History of the Insurrection in the Four Western Counties of Pennsylvania* (Spartanburg: Reprint Co., 1984), pp. 107-108.

(15) Letter John Webster to John Neville, August 2, 1794, *John Neville Papers*, Letter Book 1796-1798, Microfilm P-273, Carnegie Library of Pittsburgh.

(16) Letter John Webster to John Neville, December 16, 1794, *John Neville Papers*.

(17) Letter John Webster to John Neville, June 17, 1795, *John Neville Papers*.

(18) Thomas P. Slaughter, *The Whiskey Rebellion: Frontier Epilogue to the American Revolution* (New York: Oxford University Press, 1986), p. 111; Leland D. Baldwin, *Whiskey Rebels: The Story of a Frontier Uprising* (Pittsburgh: University of Pittsburgh Press, 1967), p. 161, 163.

(19) Linn and Egle, p. 479, 485; Franklin Ellis, ed., *History of Fayette County, Pennsylvania with Biographical Sketches* (Philadelphia: L .H. Everts & Co., 1882), p. 808.

(20) Historic Resource Study, Friendship Hill National Historic Site, September, 1981, pp. 89-90.

(21) Franklin Ellis, ed., *History of Fayette County, Pennsylvania with Biographical Sketches* (Philadelphia: L. H. Everts & Co., 1882), p. 593.

(22) Henry Adams, *The Life of Albert Gallatin* (New York: Peter Smith, 1943), p. 148; Microfilm M986 Reel 1, U. S. vs. Thomas Gaddis, May 9, 1795.

(23) Letter Benjamin Wells to John Neville, April 11, 1800, *John Neville Papers*

(24) R. Eugene Harper, p. 226.

(25) Slaughter, pp. 199-200; Baldwin, pp. 193-194; Ellis, pp. 615-616; *William and Mary College Quarterly Historical Magazine,* Vol. XI, July 1902, "A Diary Kept by Dr. Robert Wellford, of Fredericksburg, Virginia, during the March of the Virginia Troops to Fort Pitt to Suppress the Whiskey Insurrection in 1794."

(26) Jesse Calvin Cross, *Ephraim Jackson and his Descendants 1684-1960* (1961), p. 77.

(27) George D. Albert, ed., *History of the County of Westmoreland with Biographical Sketches* (Philadelphia: L. H. Everts & Co., 1882), pp. 207-212.

(28) Stotz, pp. 73-77, 144-145.

(29) Mary E. Persoll, Bess Dailey Winchell, Ernest F. Carter, *Early Days in Rostraver* (West Newton, Pa.: The Times-Sun, 1949), pp. 66, 72.

(30) Stotz, p. 31; Charles M. Stotz, *Drums in the Forest* (Pittsburgh: Historical Society of Western Pennsylvania, 1958), p. 177; Point Park Commission, Report Pt. 1, Pittsburgh, Pa., December 31, 1943; George T. Fleming, *Fleming's Scenes of Old Pittsburgh: A Portfolio of the Past* (Pittsburgh: The Crescent Press, 1932), pp. 11-13.

(31) Oliver Wolcott, *Letter from the Secretary of the Treasury Accompanying his Report on the Petition of Benjamin Wells, referred to him 1st ultimo: and the Counter Petition of Sundry Inhabitants of Fayette County* (1800), Transappalachian Room, Waynesburg College, pp. 6-12.

(32) *History of Allegheny County, Pennsylvania*, Part I (Chicago: A. Warner & Co., 1889), p 153.

(33) Chadwick A. Harp, "The Tax Collector of Bower Hill," *Pennsylvania Heritage,* Vol. XVIII, No. 4, Fall, 1992, p. 26; *John Neville Papers*; Walter Kidney, *A Guide to Allegheny Cemetery* (Pittsburgh: Pittsburgh History and Landmarks Foundation, 1990), p. 76.

(34) Hugh H. Brackenridge, *Incidents of the Insurrection in the Western Parts of Pennsylvania in the year 1794* (Philadelphia: John M'Culloch, 1795), pp. 25-26.

(35) Baldwin, pp. 241-242.

(36) Findley, pp. 56, 81; Baldwin, pp. 52, 82, 95; James P. McClure, "The Ends of the American Earth: Pittsburgh and the Upper Ohio Valley to 1795" (Ph.D. dissertation, The University of Michigan, 1983), p. 580.

(37) Brackenridge, p. 19; Washington County Will Book, Vol 5, p. 491.

(38) Noah Thompson, *History of Union Township—Surrounding Area and the Early Settlers* (Canonsburg: G. Whitaker Printing, 1976), p. 123.

(39) Baldwin, p. 49.

(40) Samuel M'Harry, *The Practical Distiller, or, An Introduction to Making Whiskey, Gin, Brandy, Spirits, etc., of Better Quality, and in Larger Quantities, than Produced by the Present Mode of Distilling from the Produce of the United States* (Harrisburg: John Wyeth, 1809); Rudolph Huffman patented 458 acres on the waters of the Pigeon Creek in 1787. By 1793 he was assessed with 360 acres, a gristmill, and a distillery.

(41) Samuel P. Bates, *History of Greene County, Pennsylvania* (Chicago: Nelson, Rishforth & Co., 1888), pp. 508-509; Slaughter, pp. 93-95.

(42) Nannie L. Fordyce, *Life and Times of Rev. John Corbly and Genealogy* (Washington, Pa.: published by compiler), p. 36.

(43) Ibid., p. 34.

(44) Louis M. Waddell, "Historical Sketch of Greene County, Pennsylvania," *Pennsylvania Heritage*, Vol. II, No. 5, December 1976, p. 6.

(45) Linn and Egle, pp. 479, 501.

(46) Microfilm M986 Reel 1, U.S. vs. William Crawford.

(47) Wall, p. 19; *The Papers of Albert Gallatin*, Washington County list of representatives.

Photo Credits

From top to bottom, left to right: Cover November 13, 1812 *Pittsburgh Gazette, Gallatin Iconography*, Albert Eugene Gallatin (privately printed, 1934), Westmoreland Museum of Art; 2 Carnegie Library, Pittsburgh; 5 Historical Society of Western Pennsylvania; 7 Atwater Kent Museum; 11 Carnegie Library, Pittsburgh; 16 Westmoreland Museum of Art; 18 Archives of Ulysses Grant Miller Library, Washington and Jefferson College; 21 Westmoreland Museum of Art; 23 Westmoreland Museum of Art; 25 Westmoreland Museum of Art; 26 Jerry A. Clouse; 28 Washington County Historical Society; 29 Historical Society of Western Pennsylvania; 30 Historical Society of Western Pennsylvania; 32 Pennsylvania State Archives, RG-4, Militia Accounts, Dauphin County; 33 Historical Society of Western Pennsylvania; 37 Carnegie Library, Pittsburgh; 39 Westmoreland Museum of Art; 43 Pennsylvania State Library; 54 Jerry A. Clouse; 55 Jerry A. Clouse; 56 Jerry A. Clouse; 57 Jerry A. Clouse; 59 Jerry A. Clouse; 60 Jerry A. Clouse; 67 Donald Shoaf, Jr., Thomas Gaddis Homestead National Register nomination; 62 Jerry A. Clouse; 63 Jerry A. Clouse; 64 *McKeesport Daily News*, Brush Hill National Register nomination, *Fleming's Scenes of Old Pittsburgh: A Portfolio of the Past*; 65 Jerry A. Clouse; 66 Historical Society of Western Pennsylvania; 67 Pittsburgh History and Landmarks Foundation, John Woods House National Register nomination; 68 Jerry A. Clouse; 70 Jerry A. Clouse; 71 Jerry A. Clouse, Jerry A. Clouse; 72 Landmarks Planning Inc., John Corbley Farm National Register nomination; 73 Jerry A. Clouse

Illustrations by Jerry A. Clouse.

Index

Adams, Henry p. 39
Adams, John p. 32, 41
Adams, Samuel p. 9
Addison, Alexander p. 2, 34, 63, 68, 72
Albany, Fayette Co. p. 62
Alleghenies p. 11, 14, 15, 16, 22, 36
Allegheny County p. 1, 22-25, 28, 34, 35, 39-40, 51, 64-67
American Revolution p. 3, 6, 8,9, 12-16, 21, 23-24, 26, 38, 41, 74
Anshutz, George p. 40
Antifederalist p. 22

Bache, Benjamin Franklin p. 30
Bacon, Ezekiel p. 47
Badolet, John p. 74
Bailey, Mountjoy p. 34
Baldwin, Leland p. 5
Balliard, Gilbert p. 4, 69,70
Baptists p. 8, 16,17
Barb, Miller p. 5
Barnd, Jacob p. 56
Bartlett, William p. 44
Battle of Fallen Timbers p. 14
Beazel, Capt. Matthew p. 63
Bedford p. 3, 17, 35,36, 38, 42, 51, 54
Bedford County p. 1, 25, 31, 53-54
Bedford Twp., Bedford Co. p. 55
Bentley, Sheshbazzer p. 45
Berlin p. 17, 40, 55,56
Berryhill, Alexander p. 3
Bill of Rights p. 13
Black Boys p. 19
Black Horse Tavern p. 63
Blaine, James p. 12
Boerster, Dr. Christian p. 40, 56
Boileau, Isaac p. 75
Boileau, Nathaniel p. 75
Bombach, Conrad p. 3
Bonham, William p. 46,47
Bonnet Tavern p. 54
Bonnet's Camp p. 38
Bouquet, Henry Col. p. 64
Bower Hill p. 5, 16, 25-27, 30, 65-69
Brackenridge, Henry M. p. 2, 14
Brackenridge, Hugh H. p. 2, 18, 23,28,29, 32-33, 37, 41, 53, 61-63, 67, 69-71
Braddock's Field p. 16, 18, 27-28, 36, 58, 65, 67, 73
Bradford, David p. 4, 18, 20, 23, 27, 31-33, 41, 45, 68, 70
Bradford, William p. 30, 33, 53
Bradford House p. 51, 70
British Isles p. 15
Brownsville p. 30
Brownsville meeting p. 59, 61
Brothers Valley Twp., Somerset Co. p. 56
Brumbaugh distillery p. 3
Brush Hill p. 63-64
Budd, Joseph p. 63
Budd's Ferry p. 63
Bullskin Twp., Fayette Co. p. 35

Cadle, Rev. Roland p. 72
Caldwell, Thomas p. 46
Canon, John p. 23, 45
Canonsburg p. 24
Carlisle p. 3, 12, 36-38, 40
Carlisle Gazette p. 12, 31
Carolinas p. 22
Cazenove, Theophile p. 14
Central Pennsylvania p. 2
Chambersburg p. 3, 36, 38
Chartiers Creek p. 4
Chartiers Valley p. 64
Chester County p. 16
Civil War p. 41
Clymer, George p. 21, 24, 37
Cochran, William p. 24
Collier Twp., Allegheny Co. p. 64
Community censure p. 18
Congress p. 1, 14, 19-21, 24, 32, 39, 40
Connecticut p. 27
Connellsville p. 22, 27, 60, 61
Cook, Col. Edward p. 5, 28, 45, 53, 58-59, 62
Cook, Edward, House p. 52, 59
Corbley, Rev. John p. 5, 16, 72
Corbley House p. 72
Couch, Nathaniel p. 67
Couch's Fort p. 25, 67
County Tyrone, Ireland p. 16
Coulter, Jonathan p. 28
Cowperthwaite, Lt. Col. Joseph p. 36
Coxe, Tench p. 10, 42, 57
Craig, Maj. Isaac p. 4, 25, 64
Craig, Neville B. p. 2
Crawford, Col. William p. 73
Crawford, William House p. 52, 73
Cumberland County p. 8, 19, 25, 30, 36
Cumberland Twp., Greene Co. p. 11, 73-74
Cumberland Valley p. 15

Daily, John p. 63
Daily, John, House p. 63
Dallas, Alexander J. p. 37, 38, 42
Davies, Canon Richard p. 4, 66
Deaner Funeral Home p. 58
Defibaugh, Adam p. 4, 55
Defibaugh, Casper p. 55
Defibaugh, Jacob p. 4, 55
Defibaugh, John Gottlieb p. 55
Defibaugh distillery p. 4
Defibaugh, William p. 3
Defibaugh Tavern p. 54
Democratic Society p. 16, 68
Democratic Society of Pa. p. 38
Democratic-Republican party p. 24
Devore's Ferry p. 28
Dibert, Frederick p. 55
Dibert, Frederick House p. 55
Dibert, Michael p. 55
Dibert, Scott p. 55
Distillers p. 10-11, 17-19, 22-25, 27, 28, 73
Distillery p. 10-11, 24
Distilling p. 9-11
Divers, George p. 11
Dreadful Night p. 39, 72

Drumm's Hotel p. 64
Dunbar p. 61
Dunbar Township p. 61
Dunlap, Capt. p. 72
Dusmal House p. 69

East p. 15, 17, 30, 34, 37
East Bethlehem Twp., Washington Co. p. 35
East Huntingdon Twp., Westmoreland Co. p. 27
Edgar, James p. 33, 68
Elections p. 39
Elizabeth Twp., Allegheny Co. p. 35
Ellis, Joseph p. 8
English p. 8, 15
Espy House p. 51, 54
Evli, Christian p. 56
Ewing, Alexander p. 65
Excise collectors p. 22, 39, 41, 58
Excise tax p. 8, 11, 13, 15, 19, 20-26, 32, 41,42, 66, 68
Extralegal meetings p. 18-19

Farmers p. 8-10, 13, 15, 39, 42
Faulkner, Capt. William p. 20, 45, 73
Faulkner's tavern p. 23
Fayette County p. 1, 22, 25, 27, 32, 35, 40, 52, 58-62
Federal law vs. state law p. 29-03, 41
Federal troops (army) p. 10, 17, 53, 58, 59, 67
Federalists p. 2, 3, 4, 16,17, 20, 28, 30-33, 38-39, 41-42, 68, 72
Federalist party p. 6, 24, 26, 41
Fell, Benjamin p. 63
Fells Church p. 17, 63
Fennell, Dorothy p. 5, 10, 69
Fenno, John p. 30
Findley, William p. 2, 21, 23, 37, 53, 57, 62, 69
Finleyville p. 16
Fisher, Glenna p. 55
Fletcher, John p. 56
Fletcher, Stevenson p. 9
Fordyce, Nannie p. 72
Forks Meetinghouse p. 17
Forman, Jonathan p. 47
Ft. Cumberland, Md. p. 38
Ft. Fayette p. 5, 26, 42
Ft. Pitt p. 64
Ft. Pitt Redoubt p. 64-65
Fourth Survey p. 24, 36
France p. 14, 15
Frederick, Md. p. 34
French and Indian War p. 13, 38
French Revolution p. 14, 23
Friends of Liberty p. 14, 18, 29
Friends of Order p. 18
Friendship Hill p. 59
Fries Rebellion p. 41
Frontier p. 8, 9, 13-14, 17, 22
Fulton, Alexander p. 26, 46

Gaddis, Thomas p. 46, 59-60
Gaddis, Thomas, House p. 52, 60, 62
Gallatin, Albert p. 2, 13, 22, 27, 31-34, 39, 41, 42, 45, 52,53, 58-60, 62, 74
Gallatin, Hannah p. 13
Garard's Fort p. 72
Gaston, John p. 68,69
Gaston House p.69
Gastonville p. 4
Gazette of the U.S. p. 30
General Advertiser p. 30
Genet, Edmund Charles p. 14
Genter, Anne p. 66
Georgia p. 19
German Baptists p. 56
German Brethren p. 8
German Twp., Fayette Co. p. 17, 52, 59-60
Germans p. 15, 17, 27, 55
Gillespie, Neal p. 45
Ginger Hill p. 70
Graham, Hugh, p. 59
Graham, William p. 8
Great Britain p. 8, 9, 26
Greene County p. 1, 5, 10, 11, 72-74
Greene Twp., Greene Co. p. 5
Greensboro p. 74
Greensburg p. 20, 30, 62
Gunsinghouser, John p. 56

Hagerstown, Md. p. 30, 31, 33
Hamilton, Alexander p. 2, 9, 20-22, 29,30, 32, 33, 34, 37, 41, 53, 62, 67
Hamilton, Daniel p. 19, 70
Hamilton, David p. 19, 23, 42, 68, 70
Hamilton, Col. John p. 4, 19, 45, 68-70
Hamilton, Thomas p. 46
Hamilton House p. 70
Hamilton's District Society p. 23, 69-70
Hanna, William p. 11
Harmar, Gen. Josiah p. 14, 34
Harper, R. Eugene p. 5, 10, 11, 52
Harrisburg p. 3
Hartley, Susanna p. 55
Hartley, William p. 55
Hartley Tavern/House p. 54-55
Hempfield Twp., Westmoreland Co. p. 17, 62
Holcroft, John p. 4, 27, 68-69
Howell, Gov. Richard p. 34
Hubbert, Capt. Christian p. 36
Huffman, Rudolph p. 76
Huffman Distillery p.71
Hughes, Thomas p. 73
Hughes House p. 73
Huling, Maj. John p. 46
Huntingdon County p. 34
Husband, Herman [Hormon] p. 7, 17, 42, 56, 57
Husband/Schneider House p. 57

Indians p. 9, 14, 19, 20, 35, 38, 42, 51, 72
Inspector of Revenue p. 1, 12, 25
Insurgents p. 53
Ireland p. 16, 56
Irish p. 15
Irvine, Gen. William p. 30, 34, 39
Irwin, John p. 63-64
Irwine, James p. 8

Jackson, Samuel p. 61-62
Jackson House p. 62
Jay Treaty p. 42
Jefferson, Thomas p. 6, 9, 11, 32, 42-43
Johnson, Robert p. 19, 20, 24, 45, 66
Juniata River p. 54

Kentucky p. 1, 12, 15, 22, 31, 42
Kentucky Gazette p. 15
Kiddoe, James p. 24, 65
Kirkpatrick, Maj. Abraham p. 26, 28, 42
Kline, George p. 31
Kline's Carlisle Weekly Gazette p. 31
Koegler, Karen p. 52-53

Landless p. 18
Large distillery p. 11
Lee, Gov. Henry p. 22, 33, 38-40, 54, 58, 68, 73
Lemon, James p. 10
Lennox, U.S. Marshal David p. 24-25, 42, 65
Liberty pole p. 30, 34, 38, 53-55, 59, 60, 61
Lincoln, Abraham p. 41
Lobb's Cemetery p. 40, 67
Lobb's Run p. 40
Long, Frederick p. 56
Louisiana p. 27
Lucas, George p. 55
Lyle, Peter p. 4, 5
Lynn, John p. 24
Lysenberger, Nicholas p. 56

Maclay, Sen. William p. 19
Madison, James p. 42
Marshall, James p. 18, 23, 45
Marshall, Thomas p. 42
Martin, Betsey p. 66
Maryland p. 3, 19, 36, 38, 54
Massachusetts p. 7
McComb, Thomas p. 45
McConnell, Alexander p. 4
McConnell, Irk p. 4
McCook, Henry p. 4
McCulloch, John p. 22
McDonald, John p. 23
McFarlane, Andrew p. 28, 67
McFarlane, James p. 16, 26, 28, 67-69
McFarlane's Ferry p. 63
McKean, Thomas p. 30, 34
McMillan, Rev. John p. 16, 68, 71
McMillan Academy p. 71
McVay, B.F. p. 4
Meason, Isaac p. 35, 53, 61-62
Methodists p. 16, 17, 21, 63
Middlesex p. 36
Mifflin, Gov. Thomas p. 29, 30, 34, 36, 37, 56
Mifflin Twp., Allegheny Co. p. 11, 24, 26
Military hospitals p. 41
Militia p. 18, 21-22, 27, 29, 33-34, 36
Miller, Oliver p. 25
Miller, Oliver, House p. 65
Miller, William p. 25, 65
Mingo Creek p. 19, 27, 36, 68-69
Mingo Creek association p. 20, 23, 68

Mingo Creek Democratic Society p. 23, 68, 69
Mingo Creek meeting p. 27, 67
Mingo Creek Presbyterian Church p. 4, 26, 68-70
Mingo Creek Society p. 26
Minor, John p. 72
Mitchell, John p. 40
Mississippi River p. 12, 14, 15, 42
Monongahela country p. 10
Monongahela River p. 12, 15, 16, 22, 31, 35, 61-63, 74
Monongahela Valley p. 9, 11, 65
Monongahela whiskey p. 12
Morgan, Gen. Daniel p. 40
Morrison's Cove p. 3
Mt. Braddock p. 61
Mountz, Maj. Caleb p. 35
Muddy Creek p. 16
Myerstown, Lebanon Co. p. 36

Naugle, Jacob p. 55
Natchez p. 12
National debt p. 21
Neville, John, Gen. p. 4, 5, 22, 23, 25-26, 28, 39, 57, 58, 61, 64-66
Neville, Presley p. 66
Neville connection p. 2, 67
Neville House p. 25-27, 42, 51, 53, 64, 66
Neville's Excise List p. 11
New Jersey p. 14, 36-38, 54
New Orleans p. 12
Newville, Pa. p. 30
North Carolina p. 7, 19
Northumberland p. 36
Northwest p. 42
Nottingham Twp., Washington Co. p. 68-69

O'Hara, James p. 65
Ohio Co., Virginia p. 31, 40
Ohio River p. 11-13, 15, 42
Ohio Valley p. 7, 8
Old St. Luke's Episcopal Church p. 66, 67
Overholt distillery p. 11

Paine, Thomas p. 17
Parkinson, Benjamin p. 45, 68
Parkinson's Ferry p. 38-40, 68, 69
Parkinson's Ferry meeting (1) p. 5, 8, 25, 31-33, 56, 59, 61, 73, 74
Parkinson's Ferry meeting (2) p. 37
Parkinson's Ferry meeting (3) p. 39
Paterson, William p. 41
Peace commission p. 29
Peace commissioners p. 30, 32, 33, 35, 36, 38, 53
Penn, Gov. John p. 13
Pennsylvania Assembly p. 13, 32, 36
Pennsylvania Commissioners p. 32-34
Pennsylvania House of Representatives p. 32
Pennsylvania militia p. 34
Pennsylvania-Virginia rivalry p. 13
Peterkin, William p. 40, 46
Peters, Judge Richard p. 41, 56
Peters Creek p. 16
Peterson, Gabriel p. 63
Philadelphia p.13, 15, 16, 19, 24, 25, 28,

34, 35, 40, 52
Philips, Rev. David p. 16, 25, 42, 45, 63
Philson, Robert p. 56
Philson-Fletcher Store/House p. 56
Pigeon Creek p. 66
Pinckney Treaty p. 42
Pittsburgh p. 2, 14, 18-20, 23, 28, 31, 36, 38-40, 42, 52
Pittsburgh Gazette p. 12, 18, 22, 31, 35, 64
Pittsburgh meeting (conference) p. 33, 58, 74
Political elites p. 17-18, 29
Porter, Robert, trial p. 45, 47
Presbyterians p. 8, 16, 17
Prisoners p. 40
Providence Twp., Bedford Co. p. 54

Queen, John p. 47
Quemahoning Twp., Somerset Co. p. 28, 57
Quigley, James p. 47

Rabb, Andrew p. 59-60, 62
Rabb, Andrew, House p. 52, 60
Randolph, Edmund p. 20, 21, 29
Rawle, William p. 24, 41
Reading p. 3
Reagan, Philip p. 27, 57, 64
Redick, David p. 37, 68
Redstone Creek p. 61
Redstone Old Fort p. 19, 32
Redstone Presbytery p. 16
Redstone Twp., Fayette Co. p. 52
Reed, John p. 16, 26
Reel's Corner p. 39
Referendum p. 34, 35-36
Regionalism p. 13-14, 34
Rehobeth Cemetery p. 58
Republican party p. 6, 24, 30, 68
Revenue Act of 1794 p. 24
Richmond, William p. 22
Robertson, John p. 45
Robinson, George p. 28
Robinson Township, Allegheny Co. p. 65
Ross, James p. 30, 35, 38
Ross, Robert p. 59
Rostraver Twp., Westmoreland Co. p. 62-63
Rowland, Jonathan p. 60
Rye p. 9, 10

St. Clair, Gen. Arthur p. 14
St. Clair Township, Allegheny Co. p. 22, 53, 67
St. Clair Township, Bedford Co. p. 4
St. Luke's Episcopal Church p. 4
Salem Baptist Church p. 63
Salem Twp., Westmoreland Co. p. 44
Sampson, William p. 63
Schenley, Mary p. 64
Schneider, Adam p. 57
Scotch-Irish p. 4, 8, 15, 17, 36, 45, 53, 56, 59
Scott, James p. 16
Scull, John p. 3, 31, 63
Settlers p. 14
1798 Direct Tax p. 11, 52
Seybert, Adam p. 10
Seyfert, Capt. Conrad p. 36

Shade Twp., Somerset Co. p. 39
Shawhan, Robert p. 22
Shays' Rebellion p. 7, 27
Shaysites p. 8
Sideling Hill p. 19
Slaughter, Thomas p. 5
Smilie, John p. 21, 22, 45, 53
Smilie, Robert p. 22
Smith, Charles p. 39
Smith, James p. 19
Smith, Joseph p. 16
Smith, Russell p. 64
Smith Twp., Washington Co. p. 35
Snake Spring Valley Twp., Bedford Co. p. 55
Society of Friends p. 61
Somerset County p. 1, 8, 17, 55-58
Somerset Twp., Washington Co. p. 11, 71
Sons of Liberty p. 40
South Huntingdon Twp., Westmoreland Co. p. 11, 64
Southeastern Pennsylvania p. 13-14
Southwestern Pennsylvania p. 1-3, 10, 15, 18, 51, 53, 61
Spain p. 9, 15
Stamp Act p. 8
Standing Committee p. 33, 35
Stevens, S.K. p. 12
Stills p. 10-12, 34, 39
Storer, Elizabeth p. 69
Storer, Thomas p. 69
Stotler, Samuel p. 39
Stotz, Charles p. 52, 63
Stoystown p. 57, 58
Strabane Township, Washington Co. p. 10, 71
Strickland, William p. 9
Strup, Sergeant p. 36
Supreme Court p. 29
Susquehanna River p. 13
Swiss p. 15

Tannehill, Josiah p. 45
Tannehill's tavern p. 20
Tar and Feathering p. 20, 24
Taxes p. 6
Tennessee p. 15
Thelan, David p. 3
Tom the Tinker p. 4, 26-28, 32, 69
Toulmin, Henry p. 12
Treason p. 27, 28, 41
Treaty of Greenville p. 42
Trial in vicinage p. 25
Trials of rebels p. 27, 31, 40
Troops p. 36-38, 40
Tully letters p. 30, 33
Tyrone Twp., Fayette Co. p. 35

Ulster p. 15
Union Furnace p. 61
Union Township, Fayette Co. p. 60
Uniontown p. 27, 30, 34, 39, 59-60
U.S. Circuit Court p. 1
U.S. Commissioners p. 33-34, 36
U.S. Constitution p. 6, 7, 13, 29, 40-41
U.S. House of Representatives p. 23
U.S. Marshal p. 1, 12
Unity Twp., Westmoreland Co. p. 36, 62

Virginia p. 19, 22, 36, 38, 54, 67

Wadington, David p. 36
Walker, Isaac p. 65
Walker-Ewing House p. 64-65
Wansey, Henry p. 9
War of the Regulation p. 7, 17
Washington, George p. 1, 2, 3, 4, 6, 8, 9, 14, 17, 20-23, 25, 27, 29, 33, 34, 36, 37, 38, 40, 41, 54, 55, 66, 68
Washington, William Augustine p. 47
Washington administration p. 22, 29
Washington cabinet p. 29
Washington County p. 1, 8, 10, 22, 24, 25, 28, 35, 39, 40, 61, 68-71
Washington County militia p. 22
Washington Democratic Society p. 23, 27
Washington town p. 20, 30, 40, 51, 68, 70
Washington Twp., Fayette Co. p. 52
Watermelon Army p. 18
Wayne, Gen. Anthony p. 14, 34
Webster, John p. 28, 57, 58, 64
Wellford, Dr. Robert p. 61, 62
Wells, Benjamin p. 20, 22, 23, 27, 57, 59-61
Wells, John p. 27
Welsh p. 15
Wentz, Colonel p. 36
West p. 6, 15, 17, 25, 26, 29, 30-31, 34
West Bethlehem Twp., Washington Co. p. 35
Westerners p. 14, 30
Western country p. 15, 21, 28, 36, 37
Western Pennsylvania p. 5, 10, 13-14, 20, 72
Western riots p. 30
Westmoreland County p. 1, 17, 21, 22, 25, 28, 35, 40, 62-64
Westsylvania p. 15
Wheatfield Twp., Westmoreland Co. p. 35
Whipple, Abraham p. 44
Whisker, Vaughn p. 3, 37
Whiskey p. 9, 10, 12, 14, 36
Whiskey, Captain p. 18
Whiskey Boys p. 3, 18
Whiskey Insurrection p. 4
Whiskey Point p. 31
Whiskey Rebellion Task Force p. 1, 50
Whiskey Rebels p. 8, 10, 22, 33, 34, 40
Whiteley Creek p. 5
Wigle (Vigol), Philip p. 22, 27, 40
Wilkins, Charles p. 12
Wilkins, John p. 12
Wilson, Adam p. 59, 61
Wilson, James p. 29
Wisegarver, George p. 55, 57, 58
Wolcott, Oliver p. 75
Woods, John p. 53, 67
Woods, John, House p. 64, 67
Woodville p. 66-67
Wray, John p. 46
Wrenshall House p. 66

Yeates, Jasper p. 30, 33, 53
Yellow fever epidemic p. 22, 31
Yohogania County Courthouse p. 67
York p. 41
Youghiogheny River p. 15, 16, 22, 35, 62, 63
Young, John p. 8

Zimmerman, Salomi p. 56

MITCHELL COLLEGE LIBRARY
437 PEQUOT AVENUE
NEW LONDON, CT 06320

```
E          CLOUSE, JERRY A.
315
.C57
1994       THE WHISKEY REBELLION: SOUTHWE
           PENNSYLVANIA'S FRONTIER PEOPLE
```

DATE DUE

GAYLORD / PRINTED IN U.S.A.